Marines Don't Cry

MARINES DON'T CRY

Delivering the Message at All Costs

Second Edition

One man's walk around the world
for children and world peace—
six continents, over fifty-two million steps,
spanning more than two decades.

DANNY GARCIA & JACKIE C. GARCIA

Global Walk Publishing

St. Augustine

MARINES DON'T CRY

Delivering the Message at All Costs

 GLOBAL WALK

ISBN 979-8-218-29113-6 paperback
ISBN 979-8-218-29466-3 ebook
Library of Congress Control Number: 2023919055

Cover Design by:
Chuck Burke

Interior Design by:
Chris Treccani
www.3dogcreative.net

Cover Photography by:
Gay Colleypriest

Second Edition 2023

To God,
this is His book.
To our parents and our family
To veterans, first responders, and their families
To our warrior dog, Shalom

Semper Fidelis (April 2021)

CONTENTS

Part I   **1**

Chapter 1:   Molded in the Concrete Jungle   3
Chapter 2:   Once a Marine, Always a Marine   21
Chapter 3:   Peace, Love, and Music   33
Chapter 4:   Return to the Corps and Human Relations Fame   49
Chapter 5:   Lost—Having It All, Having Nothing   67
Chapter 6:   The Pope and *The Child*   87
Chapter 7:   "You Must Choose Now"   95
Chapter 8:   "God, Give Me Life"—
              Emerging from the Crucible   117

Part II   **127**

Introduction   127
Chapter 9:   First 3,500 Miles Plus, Walks in the US   131
Chapter 10:   Marines—Hands Across the Sea   155
Chapter 11:   Cousin Bruce, Music Man   181
Chapter 12:   Walking for Children Around the World   189
Chapter 13:   Taken Hostage in Gaza   207
Chapter 14:   Transparency and Vulnerability—
              A Word about PTSD   219

Conclusion   225
About Global Walk   228
About the Coauthors   231
Endnotes   235
Contact the Coauthors   250

SPECIAL MENTION OF HEROIC MARINE

Inductee, Commando Hall of Fame (Special Forces)
Medal of Honor Nominee
Author, *Faith Through the Storm*

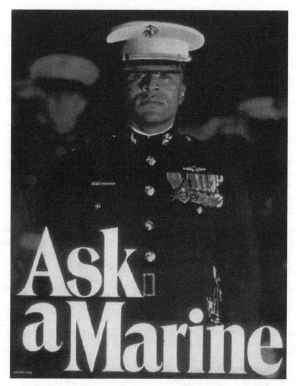

Major James, Capers, Jr., USMC (Retired)

ACKNOWLEDGMENTS

Writing this book took nearly five years. Recalling, reliving, and detailing the events was a grueling, yet incredibly rewarding experience. We believe this book will be a legacy for our children. We would like to sincerely thank the individuals who guided and encouraged us, as well as the institutions that gave us the grit to endure and persevere.

To Our Rock: We acknowledge Jesus Christ, our salvation, our hope. We can do nothing without you, and with you we can do all things. It is our faith in Jesus that propels us, that gives us strength, and that compels us to share hope. This is his book and a gift to all who read it.

To Our Parents: Jose Bilingue Garcia, Margaret Knowles Garcia, Jose Aguon Charsagua, and Dominga Rodriguez Charsagua, who have passed from this earth; left us an enduring legacy of music, service to country, and devotion; and raised servants of character and integrity. We love and honor all of you.

Those who befriended us: Rick Lonto, you gave Danny fellowship and a place to live and lay his head between walks; you were a rock of prayer. Being your best man and vice versa has been an honor. To Chris and Lisa Taliaferro, who sheltered Danny during his turmoil and heartbreak, and now after thirty years, provide vacation respite and remain our dear friends. To

Billy, William Ford, III, our loyal friend in Virginia, who always accepts us as we are. You are the real deal and a true friend. To Richard Shenk, you were there in the beginning of Danny's ministry, as close as a brother and a now our constant intercessor. We are thankful you are back in our lives. To Bruce Stephen Foster, our creative friend, you are a talented musician and artist, incredibly humble. Thank you for writing a chapter of this book and recording original music for Danny's walks; we know more music is yet to come.

Those who mentored us: We thank our mentors, many who are no longer in this world, and while associated with Danny, made an indelible impact on his life. Bud Roberts of Shell Oil, who taught him to be a proper gentleman and a public relations master; Mr. and Mrs. Alexander of Grenada, who taught him to interact and present himself as a diplomat; General Charles C. Krulak, Commandant, US Marine Corps who showed unswerving character and trust in Sgt Garcia, allowing Danny to yield noteworthy results during his time in the Corps. Col Leslie S. Miller, USAF, who literally saved Jackie's life and showed true leadership and unbounding compassion.

Those who molded us: The US Marine Corps (the few, the proud, the Marines). We especially acknowledge the brothers who served in Vietnam but did not return home. To the United States Air Force and United States Air Force Academy for the exceptional education and foundation of character and leadership afforded to Jackie to be successful in life. A special shout out to Jackie's classmates from the USAFA Class of 1985 who always have her back and continue to inspire and excel ('85 Best Alive).

Those who partnered with us: The peace-making trio of Monica Willard, Deborah Muldow, and Ann Marie Robustelli, who have known Danny for over two decades as fellow activists for peace and carry the torch with the simple prayer, "May Peace Prevail on Earth." You are always in our hearts.

Those who sponsored this book: These generous donors helped to either finance this book or provide in kind donations for promotion. We are grateful for their generosity, more so, their belief in us. Tom Day of Bugles Across America; Glenn Sandler (may he rest in peace); Bob Okun of America Salutes You; Jose Torres of Shaklee Corporation; Brad and Alisha Fairman, our friends and realtors; Douglas Sturomski of Peace Bells Foundation.

Those who put this book in print: Our first edition publisher, the Morgan James Publishing Team, who guided us as first-time authors and got our book out there. To our editor, Cortney Donelson, who is incredibly responsive, thorough, and detail oriented. Her insight into storytelling was invigorating. And for our dear friend Chuck Burke, who has blessed us with his extensive expertise in printing, graphics, and marketing, which has laid the foundation for our future of self-publishing. We can't thank you enough!

Part I

CHAPTER 1:

Molded in the Concrete Jungle

New York City was in blizzard conditions—one of the worst I was told. It was March 1945. World War II had ended in Europe and the United Nations was being born. A young Cuban musician, Jose Garcia, was focused on one thing: getting his pregnant bride through the storm and safely to the hospital. After a nail-biting taxi trip, the young couple arrived and welcomed me, Daniel Garcia, into the world on March 18, 1945. Born into the intoxicating world of a marriage between a beauty queen and a musician, I was destined to have a fascinating, glamorous life. Two years later, my sister, Linda, joined the Garcia family.

My mother, Margaret "Margie" Knowles, was beautiful and loving. My mother and father were childhood sweethearts. My father was eight years older than my mother, and he was teased about "robbing the cradle." He was handsome and charming. While many men wanted to court my mother, she only had eyes for him. His persistence won her over, and Margaret finally consented to marry him. The family hosted a beautiful wedding. They were very much in love.

Latin Roots: Afro-Cubans in Spanish Harlem

My grandparents were originally from Ybor City in Tampa, Florida. Both of my parents were born in Ybor City. In the 1930s, when the cigar industry in Tampa declined and plunged many Cubans into poverty, Afro-Cuban families made an exodus to New York City to find work. My mother was twelve years old when her family moved to New York City, where the Knowles and Garcia families settled in the area known as Spanish Harlem. The early migrants from Ybor City, Tampeños, formed a community between Lennox and Lexington Avenues from 110th Street to 115th Street—about ten blocks below the main Harlem. Our first home in New York City was an apartment house on 106th Street and Columbus Avenue. It was a bright red building four stories high with fire escapes in the back. As a child, I thought that apartment seemed so big. In reality, every room was small.

Compared to most apartments, ours was in good condition. We had windows with screens and no peeling paint. In the spring and summer, we climbed out of the windows, zipped down the fire escape to play in the yard, or scrambled up to play on the roof. I roof-hopped from building to building and ran in the streets. On the hot summer nights, we sat on the fire escape to cool off and share secrets and stories. Our main street was filled with other apartments, vendors, and a supermarket. At the junior high school, I played softball, basketball, and handball against the school walls. In the winter, we roller skated and played hockey.

Every day, I saw a flow of people in and out of the apartment building. The building manager, Mrs. Williams, lived on the first floor. She was Irish and smelled like Clorox bleach. Every day, she cleaned and scrubbed our building. Many times, Linda and I got in trouble for playing on the stairs, and Mrs. Williams would shake her fist at us as we ran and hid. Like a mother hen, Mrs. Williams tried to keep tabs on all of us. She loved my curly hair and often babysat me and let me ride my tricycle on the sidewalk in front of our building. My sister and I would slide down the hallway banister yelling "hello" to our neighbors. Everyone left their apartment doors open. We were a tight community of different nationalities. We were family. Our building was like a miniature United Nations.

Our favorite neighbor was Machito, who lived in an apartment below us. Machito would call out, "Danny come, come in! Here. Take this change." He fished in his pockets for coins then said, "Here's some money for you. Go to the movies or get ice cream."

"Gracias, Machito," I said with a huge grin as I ran to the movies.

To me, Machito was like an uncle. To the world, he was an accomplished orchestra leader. I was surrounded by musicians who visited Machito and our home to talk about music. These visitors later were acknowledged as greats in the Latin music industry. One of those legendary musicians was my father.

Jose Garcia was an Afro-Cuban percussionist, specifically a conguero (conga drummer) and bongocero (bongo drummer). He played tall, narrow, single-headed Cuban drums (the congas) and several smaller drums (bongos) that he held between his knees. Early conga drums were salvaged rum or wine barrels. Afro-Cuban musicians traditionally used these drums in genres such as conga and rumba.

Since the age of ten, as a boy living in Cuba, Jose Garcia played the congas and the bongos. My father even made his own congas, buying cow skins and the base of the drum. He prepared the conga by stretching the skin across the drum, securing the skin against the drum with metal rings, and tightening it with bolts. After it was trimmed and stretched, and before he could use it to perform, he would ignite a flame that heated the skin. The skins would stretch even more, and he masterfully created various sounds as he played. Different skins with specific thicknesses, tightened and customized, created unique tonal sounds: an indigenous Cuban skill for a Cuban musician.

My father did not read music, but he could hear and feel music as if it were part of his body and soul. When I was a young boy, my father gave me my own set of bongos and taught me how to listen to music and play by ear. He sat me down, bongos between my knees, and I mimicked his unique style. Playing the drums was natural to me. My father was handsome, young, and talented. Jose Garcia possessed a gift that would take him to extraordinary heights, and his talent added a certain seasoning to the tunes and compositions he created. Jose was one of the pioneers who introduced congas to the Latin music scene in the United States. One of my father's proudest moments was as a conguero playing at the first World's Fair in New York in 1939.

We called him "Papi" for Dad. In the Afro-Cuban music world, he was called "Bilingue" (which means bilingual) because he spoke both English and Spanish fluently. Many of the Latin musicians could only speak Spanish, so they relied on my father, who translated for them. Francisco "Machito" Grillo (the neighbor who gave me his pocket change) recognized my father's talent, and in 1941 invited my father to play in Machito's orchestra, Machito and The Afro-Cubans. Another great maestro and

Machito's brother-in-law, Mario Bauza, was the "architect of the orchestra" and, with Machito and other band members, was among the pioneers who mixed Latin and jazz compositions and created the genre known as CuBop, or Afro-Cuban jazz. For the Afro-Cubans, Mario Bauza hand-picked and "demanded percussionists who were versed in Afro-Cuban traditional music." And my father was his first bongocero.

Machito lived on the second floor of my apartment building. On Saturday nights, from our third-floor apartment, my sister Linda and I peeked through our bedroom door and watched as the two apartments became one. Men and women, old and young, would drift up and down the smoke-filled staircase all night long, creating music into the wee hours of the morning. Music was everywhere, as was dancing and alcohol. I recall fancy ladies with their bobbed hair. They held long and slender cigarette holders and tilted their chins up as the cigarette smoke floated through the air. The men smoked cigars. These dapper men were dressed in their dark suits with crisp white shirts and neckties. Their shoes shined so brightly that you could see your face in them. My sister grabbed the sheet from her bed and draped it around her shoulders. She used a stick or toothbrush as her cigarette holder, strutting around our room pretending to be a "fancy lady."

The Copa, Copacabana

My father played with many different groups and venues. We boasted to our friends that our Dad played at the famous Copacabana. When I was nine years old, I visited the iconic club on 10 E 60th Street in New York City. The club dazzled in Brazilian décor and booked many Latin-themed orchestras. The Copa was known for their chorus line, The Copacabana Girls. They had pink hair, hair turbans made of fruit, and elaborately sequined costumes.

"Danny," my mother said with lightness in her voice, "I am taking you somewhere very special to see your father play."

At that time, my father was performing with another great, Xavier Cugat. Xavier Cugat was a Spanish-American bandleader influenced by the music of Havana, Cuba. He became a leading figure in the spread of Latin music in the United States. In New York City, he was the leader of the resident orchestra at the Waldorf-Astoria before and after World War II.

My mother dressed me in my finest suit and clipped on my tie. I felt ten feet tall. Once dressed, we waited and waited for the taxi to come. I bubbled with excitement and kept jumping up and down.

"Stop that jumping," my mother scolded. "You'll get all dirty, and then we won't be able to go." So that calmed me down, for a few moments.

When the taxi pulled up in front of the "great American nightclub," the Copacabana, I could hardly contain my excitement. New Yorkers went to the Copa to party! The Copa had the best food, the best Champagne, and the best entertainment. An American singer and actress, Abbe Lane, joined us at our table. The beautiful green-eyed celebrity was married to Xavier Cugat and sang with Cugat's band. Abbe was a big fan of my father and took a special liking to me. She held me on her lap during breaks as we both watched my parents dance. When Jose and Margaret stepped on the dance floor, everyone cleared off and watched with amazement and admiration. The Garcias were a sight to behold; passionate and graceful dancers. They were a strikingly handsome couple.

Early Days of Sports and Catholic School

As a young boy, I played sports outdoors from the time the sun came up until dark. I played every sport I could: basketball, football, baseball, and stickball (hitting a rubber ball with a broomstick). I was a good athlete, often chosen first for a team. I was a good pitcher and a good three-point shooter. I couldn't get enough of playing sports.

In the muggy heat of the summer, the street was our swimming pool. We opened the fire hydrants, put a can over the spout, and splashed in the water spray. As cars drove by, we pleaded to wash them to earn some extra cash. Even if they refused, we still washed them. At night, we snuck into the community pools to swim. We also went to summer camps sponsored by the Police Athletic League (PAL) or Catholic Youth Organization (CYO). When Halloween came, we blasted off firecrackers from the rooftops and set them off from one roof to the other.

As my father became more successful, my family spent vacations on Coney Island and Orchard Beach at the Bronx Riviera, where many Hispanics met. Mami and Papi brought mounds of food. We stuffed ourselves and swam until we were exhausted.

"Jose can swim like a shark," people said of my father.

Our extended family (aunts, uncles, cousins, and grandparents) joined us at Orchard Beach. All of us lay together on blankets talking, swimming, or playing in the sand. When my father got restless, he walked around the promenade. Before long, we heard his bongos. Linda ran to see where the sound was coming from and came dashing back to the family's spot.

"It's Papi! Come and see," Linda shouted with delight and pride.

We all went toward the direction of the music and found my father playing the bongos and entertaining crowds of people. When he played, people energetically laughed and danced. We weren't financially rich, but we were rich in our love for one another. During these times, I beamed with pride for my family.

My mother worked as an IBM keypuncher (when comput-
ers still processed commands with stacks of punched cards) and
was the anchor in our family. She worked long hours, sometimes
two jobs, and then came home to cook. In a Latin family, certain
roles were defined and expected. My father expected my mother
to cook and put food on the table for everyone. My father cooked
sometimes (and he was a great cook). His favorite dish was crabs,
and he cooked his own killer sauce hot enough to make you cry.

When Linda and I were young, we played games together. We
had a linoleum floor adorned with nursery school characters like
Humpty Dumpty and Jack and Jill. She played with her dolls and
made them talk to these characters. I teased her unmercifully with
my toy soldiers until, in tears, Linda ratted me out to Mami.

My mother wanted to provide the best for her children. She
enrolled us in Holy Name of Jesus Catholic School on 96th Street
in Amsterdam, New York. Everyone seemed to be white and Irish
in this school. There were few Hispanics and even fewer Blacks.
Several of the Catholic brothers were big and strong like football
players, and they intimidated me. Soon, when I thought of going
to school, I had physical aches in the pit of my stomach. I experienced fear.

I feared discipline if my handwriting wasn't good enough.
The sisters had a way of snapping a thirty-two-inch ruler on your
knuckles to get your attention.

Discipline was a major aspect of Catholic school. Here, the
brothers and nuns instilled in me to never quit. We lived and
breathed religion, studied the church catechism, went to Mass,
etc. Our parents did not attend Mass on Sundays, but we took the
bus and went.

Because of my athletic abilities, I was a popular kid in school.
As a fifth-grader, I was the starting pitcher on the varsity fast-pitch

team. I also played infield and outfield. When I was on the mound, I always talked to God before I pitched. Looking at the batter, I sized him up, looked at his stance, and consulted the Lord.

"God, how do I pitch to him?" I questioned. "Do I pitch fast? Do I pitch slow? Do I give him a changeup? A curveball?"

The moment I asked God these questions, he answered me. I received his message and, as I wound up to throw and release the pitch, I knew the exact pitch for that batter. I had many strikeouts. I did not lose. In fact, I always won. For a while, I remember being a happy kid, even in Hell's Kitchen as a cog in the wheel of a tough neighborhood.

Hell's Kitchen

Many times, I chose to walk to and from school, unless the weather was bad. By walking, I saved bus fare and used the money for snacks. In the inner city, everyone knew that the gangs claimed certain blocks. Skin color was not the issue or how the gangs claimed territory. It was about who was the baddest and who could prove it.

It didn't matter if I was home or at school, I had to be willing to fight. In Spanish Harlem, I had to defend myself and my territory to be respected. I fought to gain and to keep respect. This is a rule of the streets; a rule of the concrete jungle.

During the mid-1950s, Spanish Harlem, or Hell's Kitchen, was diverse and had many nationalities living there. It felt like a United Nations of sorts. Often, other families invited me to their national celebrations, where I was introduced to their languages and customs. I sampled French, Spanish, Oriental, Jamaican, and Indian cuisines. I lived in an American melting pot and traveled throughout all of the boroughs of New York City. This cultural immersion was how I was able to naturally accept people of other races and cultures.

Marlon Brando in the 1954 movie *On the Waterfront* brought back vivid memories of that time and my life in Hell's Kitchen. It was volatile and violent. Older people were very friendly and looked after you; younger people drifted toward violence. The environment lured the young with promises of easy money and fame.

My father used to tell me, "You can't just be a punk and run away. You've got to fight for your rights. Pick up a stick. Here's one. Now go get the bread and don't come back without it." Papi put the stick in my hand and pointed to the door. I went out scared but ready.

My father's lifestyle as an artist, as a musician, had been taking precedence over family. His music was his life, and that life was encircled with smoking, drinking, and partying. He seemed to be away from home endlessly either rehearsing, working in recording studios, or performing late into the evening, both in New York City and abroad. Bilingue had left for Caracas, Venezuela, at one point, but returned with empty pockets and no earnings to support the family.

My mother demanded his attention and support. Time with family turned into boisterous arguments which led to physical violence. When my parents were home, they were always fighting, both verbally and physically. The weekends brought drinking and fighting. I received many mixed messages. We tried to portray ourselves as a normal family. But what is normal in Spanish Harlem? Every Friday night, we went out as a family for pizza and laughed and joked around. I often went to the movies on Saturdays, sneaking in and spending all day and night there. The movies were my escape and became my lifelong respite to get away from stress and to relax. On Sundays, my parents stayed in bed and read the newspapers while Linda and I took the bus to church.

On the other side of the coin, I have memories I cannot forget of my parents hurting each other. One night, they both had been drinking, and Mami taunted and aggravated my father. It seemed that she baited him, egging on an argument with my father. Both lost patience and reason. I vividly and painfully remember my father, in a frenzy of anger, attempting to throw my mother out of the window.

"Papi, stop!" I cried and screamed. "Let her go!"

I was afraid that my father was going to kill my mother.

I tried to pull him from behind so that he would stop hurting her. I wasn't strong enough, and he brushed me aside like a blanket. I was a little boy trying to stop a full-grown man.

"Let her go, Papi, stop it!" I cried.

Papi released my mother and she crawled backwards into the apartment. He turned around and looked at me with tears rolling down my face. I could tell that my tears hurt him.

I felt that my parents put me right into the middle of their battles. It was a painful and confusing situation to be in. Many times, my mother talked about leaving, but my sister Linda begged her to reconsider and stay. Linda was very close to my father; she didn't want him to leave. She always wanted to be with him and thought things would be OK. Linda tried to be the peacekeeper, and she was devoted to my parents. I wanted to get away from both because I felt so hurt and discouraged.

Mami periodically sent us to her parents in Harlem, where Nana, my great-grandmother, also lived. Nana Juana Armenteo was born in Havana, Cuba, and was a large, dark-skinned woman. Nana loved me and protected me from the war zone in my home. With Nana, I experienced peace, joy, and laughter. I remember her sitting and looking out her third-floor window and calling to the fruit vendors in the street. I sat on her lap and listened to her stories as she smoked her Cuban cigar and drank her half gallon of Gallo wine. She taught me how to play cards and gamble with the best of them.

Because of my parents' marital problems, I eventually went to live with my mother's parents (Ernest and Christina Knowles) in Harlem—251 W 112th Street. My Grandfather Ernest was white (and looked like Erol Flynn), and my Grandmother Christina was fair-skinned. She spoke several languages, including Italian, fluently. They lived in Harlem at a time of prejudice and when white people were not welcome in Harlem. However, the Knowles were liked and respected in that community, even though it was a predominantly Black neighborhood. Linda, determined to help my parents, stayed behind and did not move to Harlem.

Fight to Survive, Fight for Respect

At the age of ten and in the Black neighborhood of Harlem, I was now the kid with the lightest complexion. In that part of Harlem, I was a "mulatto," someone of mixed Black and Caucasian parents and having a light-brown skin color. The neighborhood kids harassed me and called me "a spick." I had to fight for everything. When I went downstairs, a bunch of guys were typically waiting to jump me. I had to fight to get past them to go to the store to buy a loaf of bread; otherwise, they took my money. There were so many of them bullying me. I tried to ignore the pecking and haggling. I learned quickly that avoiding the bullies only encouraged and escalated their harassment.

One day, the Black kids ambushed me in the streets. I can't remember how many of them attacked me. The gang jumped me and pounded me with punches. Then, something welled up in me.

I snapped and exploded with rage on the bullies. I fought back, swinging wildly at anyone near me. I had one of the bullies pinned to the ground, and I kept hitting him in the face with my fists. I was out of control.

Someone then jumped in. It was a man who grabbed me by the shoulders and pulled me off the boy on the ground. He made me sit down until I could regain my senses.

"Cool down now," the man said. With his hand, he signaled it was over.

I breathed hard, my chest heaving until I had my composure back. My rage subsided, and the bullies cringed in pain. At that moment, I gained respect and a reputation in the neighborhood. This is a rule of the streets: fight for respect.

Soon I was accepted and became the leader of the pack. I kept looking for someone I could relate to, someone who could understand me. I found acceptance in the streets and with my own gang. I became a war counselor and negotiated with other gangs. This street knowledge helped me survive in Hell's Kitchen.

As a teenager, I moved to Brooklyn in an area called Williamsburg (Bedford Stuyvesant) with my mom. I went back and forth from my parents' to my Aunt and Uncles' home. Everywhere I lived I walked. Sometimes, my mother would give me cab fare, but I wouldn't use it. I would pocket the cash and just walk.

Sports and inner-city community programs helped keep me occupied through my teen years. I played in Columbia University's Little League in Morningside Park. I also played in neighborhood leagues, school leagues, and leagues with grown men. They all wanted me because I was a great softball pitcher and never lost. My love of sports and athletic ability rescued me. If I hadn't had athletics, I would have been a statistic—dead or in jail, a victim of the streets.

First Mentor, Uncle Victor

God provided other family members to love me and care for me. I had stayed close to my Aunt ("Titi" in Spanish) Red and Uncle Victor and moved into an attic room in their home in Hollis, Queens. Titi had one daughter and always wanted a son. I remember that once Titi Red even asked my mother if she could adopt me. Titi Red and Uncle Victor paid attention to me and were involved in my life. They took me camping, to the beach, and to the drive-in movies. On Sunday mornings, Uncle Victor and I woke up early and cooked chicken and eggs for breakfast. It was a private time for us to talk about everything.

My Uncle Victor was a Golden Gloves champion and pro boxer who won his first fifteen professional fights with no losses. Because he "cut" (swelled and bled) very easily during his boxing bouts, my Titi, out of concern, insisted that he quit boxing. Uncle Victor retired and stayed close to boxing and boxing trainers. Uncle Victor loved me as a son he never had. Because I was an exceptional athlete, he wanted me to box as well. He introduced me to his trainer, Victor Valley, who taught me how to box at Bobby Gleason's gym in the Bronx. The odor of men's sweat greeted me as I walked into the gym. Bodies glistened and muscles rippled as the boxers punched the heavy and light bags and shadowboxed while looking at themselves in the mirror. As a sixteen-year-old young man, I couldn't wait to be like them.

Victor Valley taught me the art of boxing. I learned how to jab with my left arm while my right arm was tied to my side. I learned movements on how to slip a punch, bob and weave, and dance in the ring. I learned combinations of jabs, right crosses, and left hooks. Whatever tactics and moves were used in the ring sent a message to my opponent. I had to read my opponent's punches as well. Flowing between offense and defense became second nature to me. Victor Valley prepared me for the Golden Gloves Tournament in New York City. My Uncle Victor was so proud that I was about to follow in his footsteps as a boxer.

When he thought I was ready, Victor Valley allowed me to spar with pro boxer Bennie "Kid" Paret, who was also Cuban. It was my first fight in a ring, and Benny was easy on me. Shortly after my sparring with Bennie, he had a championship match scheduled with Emile Griffith, who lived across the street from us in Queens. Tragically, Bennie was knocked out in the Welterweight title match with Emile Griffith on March 24, 1962, and died ten days later.

US Marine Corps Recruiters

During one of my training sessions, two Marine Corps recruiters saw me in the gym. One of the recruiters was in a sharp uniform—dress blues.

He said, "How would you like to join the Marines and fight with us? We are looking for a few good men."

It was an offer I couldn't refuse. I was about to turn seventeen. By this time, I had moved out to live on my own. I was staying with an older friend and working in a deli. I was bored and tired of jumping from one house or school to another. School didn't interest or challenge me. I quit school in eleventh grade without a high school diploma. I felt I was always searching for something, perhaps the *Leave it to Beaver* family I never had. I needed a feeling of peace and security and had already drifted away from the church.

I was looking to belong. Sports saved me as a boy, and I saw the Marines as an escape from the concrete jungle.

In those days (1962), if a recruit was not yet eighteen years of age, he had to have both parents' signatures to enlist.

My mother said, "Honey, this is dangerous. They're always fighting; they're always going to war."

"This is what I want to do," I insisted.

My parents eventually did agree and provided parental consent. This was maybe the last time they ever agreed on anything concerning their son, which was to allow him to join military service in the Marine Corps.

Looking back on my family and childhood, I never really knew my father. It seemed he was always in recording sessions or traveling internationally. We didn't talk much, and when we did, it was nothing of importance. He rarely asked about me. He asked me to go to the store to get him packs of Pal Mal cigarettes. We did not have a strong bond or a connection. This fatherly absence impacted me throughout my life. Nonetheless, I loved and admired my father and always wanted a meaningful relationship with him. I believed he loved me but did not know how to show me his love.

The concrete jungle molded me to think, "I can't quit." In all the trauma and pain that comes from living in the ghetto, I learned to survive. As a boy, I certainly knew about God, and my Catholic schooling taught me to be afraid of God and mortal sin. I talked to Him, and he answered me.

I know that God was with me every step of the way. He protected me and kept me strong. He is the one who gave me the strength and courage to do what I had to do to help my mother. He was there as I fought the fight that would earn me the respect of the neighborhood gangs.

Today, I truly do thank God for the difficult times I endured. The trials molded me and drew me closer to Him, causing me to depend totally on Him whether in the classroom, in the streets, in sports, and even at home.

The Catholic Church gave me discipline and a never-quit mindset. This prepared me for the US Marine Corps. God opened the door for me to enlist in the Marine Corps and to experience the family I was searching for.

I left the war of the concrete jungle, molded in the streets, and was being prepared for another war zone. God was always with me; I was in the hands of the master potter.

CHAPTER 2:

Once a Marine, Always a Marine

May 1962. A bus full of recruits from New York City is headed to Parris Island, South Carolina, for Marine Corps boot camp. I was on that bus. I had left my old life and was ready for a new life.

Once I made my mind up to do something, I saw it through. I watched war movies and wanted to be a warrior. Both the Air Force and the Army tried to recruit me, but I wanted to be part of the elite Marine Corps. When I left New York City, I felt the stress of family instability being lifted from my shoulders.

On the long bus ride south, I contemplated the current events of the time. President Kennedy had banned all trade with Cuba and set up a blockade. The US had been performing nuclear tests in Nevada. The Soviet Union and the US exchanged prisoners: U-2 pilot Francis Gary Powers for Russian spy Rudolf Abel.

I wondered how those international events had anything to do with me, a seventeen-year-old in prime physical condition.

Marine Corps Boot Camp

The bus from New York City arrived at boot camp in the evening, maybe 9:00 p.m. As soon as the bus stopped, the chaos began. I heard screaming outside of the bus.

"Get off the bus! Line up outside!" shouted a Marine Corps drill instructor (DI).

There was no cordial welcome, no warm handshake, no polite offers of assistance. We were boots (new recruits), and we knew nothing. Most of the guys that arrived with me were college-aged, grown white men. I was the youngest and had turned seventeen years old just two months earlier. There was one other recruit like me—a white kid from the streets of Philadelphia. We didn't have a college education, but we had the toughness of the streets.

We were ushered inside the building in front of us, and the indoctrination began. We were herded like sheep to the barracks (the sleeping quarters). We couldn't talk or look at anyone.

"Claim an empty rack and go to sleep," they told us.

Minutes after I fell asleep (at least it seemed like minutes), I heard a metal trash can loudly crashing and bouncing through the middle of the bay. I jolted awake and jumped out of my rack. Then I heard the DI yelling commands.

"Get out of your racks and stand at attention!" bellowed Sergeant (Sgt) Hendricks.

Sgt Hendricks was the junior drill instructor. His hat reminded me of Smokey Bear. He was short in stature; a thin and lean African American man. He looked angry, and his mission was to intimidate the boots. Everyone scrambled out of bed and snapped themselves upright to attention so they were facing front, eyes forward. I stood erect, elbows pinned to my side, completely still. Sgt Hendricks walked by me. I instinctively and momentarily glanced down at him.

Sgt Hendricks responded immediately, "Keep your eyeballs straight, boot!"

Then, *pow*! He punched me in my gut, just like in the movies. It was an unexpected blow that took the wind out of me. I hunched over and caught my breath. After a few seconds, I stood back up at attention with no complaint. I had taken punches before. I had to be tough and keep my mouth shut, I knew that much. I did not show weakness and kept looking straight ahead, just like I was told. The DIs knew I was different.

Marine Corps boot camp training lasted twelve weeks. We had a daily routine: get up, clean up, get chow, get uniforms, get your rifle, get your manuals. Train, train, train. Every day was exhausting, and by the end of the day, we wanted to hit the sack and get a bit of sleep. We were taught how to wear a uniform and how to walk with military bearing and proper posture. We ran every day and were taught to march in formation as a military unit, in step and in unison.

"Heel, toe, arm swing, six to the front, three to the rear," chanted the recruits.

We marched. We ran to Jody calls—a call and response cadence that keeps everyone together and instills camaraderie. We learned the sixteen-count manual of arms, how to stand with the rifle, how to salute with the rifle, how to run with the rifle. The M-1 rifle was our companion; a sturdy and dependable semi-automatic. We slept with it, cleaned it, took it apart blindfolded, and put it back together blindfolded. The M-1 was our treasured weapon, and we learned to "fix bayonet" (attach a bayonet to the top of the M-1). "Fix bayonet" was a command to go into hand-to-hand combat with the enemy in close range. We were trained to be killers.

Every Marine is trained to be an infantryman. We all spent time on the firing range for target practice to qualify as an expert, sharpshooter, or marksman.

During deep-water training, the DIs ushered us into an indoor pool area. There were several instructors in charge of water survival training.

"Is there anybody who doesn't know how to swim?" they asked the group. I did not respond.

The instructors explained what we needed to do. We were to dive into the deep end of the pool with all of our gear and come up with nothing but our boots and rifle. I was scared but didn't show it. I wasn't going to let them think I was a coward. Three of us at a time stepped toward the edge of the pool. As I waited for my turn, my mind raced.

"If I go down, since I can't swim, how am I going to come back up?" I asked myself.

At the command of the instructors, each group of three plunged into the deep end of the pool.

"Jump!"

I took a deep breath and dove in the water. Underwater, I stripped off my clothing and gear and surfaced to the top. I floundered and sputtered, slapping wildly at the water trying not to sink. Another DI on the side immediately extended a pole over the water for me to cling to. I grabbed it, and they dragged me to the side of the pool.

"Garcia! You mean to tell me you can't swim? You know who would be responsible if you drowned and died?" the DIs and the water survival instructors fumed at me.

"Why didn't you tell me you *can't swim*, Garcia?"

"Sir! I was just doing what you told me to do!" I gasped.

Sgt Hendricks roared, "Get out of the water!"

I was embarrassed, and everyone was looking at me. Who would be crazy enough to jump into the deep end while not being able to swim? Sgt Hendricks didn't say it, but as he looked at me, I sensed that he was telling me something:

"You've got guts."

The DIs gave me a leadership job: a house mouse. The house mouse ran messages for the DI, passed DI instructions to the boots, took care of the barracks, and readied the boots before the DIs arrived. Not every boot could survive the basic training regimen. The wash-out (or attrition) rate during boot camp was 50 percent or higher during my era. Parris Island was no vacation spot, either. Swamps surrounded the island, and the swamps were full of alligators, snakes, and quicksand. There was no escape. There were stories of recruits who ventured out into the swamp and did not return.

During the summer months, South Carolina was hot and humid. Some boots would pass out under the brutal rays of the sun.

After twelve weeks of intense training, I completed boot camp. I was a Marine. I made it to boot camp graduation. This was big for me. No one could ever take this accomplishment from me, ever. I was molded physically and mentally. Whatever they did to me, I took it. If I got through boot camp, I thought, I could get through anything.

I made it through as a seventeen-year-old kid. I became a man.

Boot camp taught me how to react to any given combat situation without thinking. We were trained and licensed to kill. Marines were conditioned to do what must be done and to do it quickly. The Marine that jumps on a live grenade to save his buddy doesn't think about it. He just does it and sacrifices his life for his fellow Marines.

The Marine Corps motto "Semper Fidelis" is Latin for "always faithful." The motto is ingrained in every Marine. Marines say "Semper Fi" for short. We are faithful to the Corps, to our fellow Marines, to God, and our country.

Marines do not fear. Marines don't quit.

Marines look after each other. Marines are comrades and family.

Marines don't cry.

For the graduation ceremony, family members eagerly participated. Unfortunately, my family did not attend. Afterward, I went back to Brooklyn for three weeks of leave. I arrived home in my tropical uniform looking fit and poised. The neighborhood welcomed me as a hero.

My mother beamed and said, "Danny loves his Marine Corps."

When leave ended, my next training stop was Camp Geiger, North Carolina, for advanced infantry training. Afterward, I was stationed at Marine Corps Base Camp Lejeune, North Carolina, with a military occupational specialty (MOS) of wireman and switchboard operator. Every Marine was considered a rifleman first, MOS assignment second.

Deployed Out to Sea

At Camp Lejeune, I settled into my barracks and performed my duties. My unit was prepared to go at a moment's notice. One day, my commanding officer announced that we were shipping out.

"Get your gear together, get outside on the vehicles," said the First Sergeant.

I grabbed my rifle, my pack, everything in sight, and the next thing I knew, I was on a ship. I didn't know where I was going. All I knew was that I was on an APA—a troop carrier—with approximately 3,000 Marines headed out to sea.

I never forgot my first assignment. It was October 1962. There I was, fresh out of combat training and on my first mission. I was at the bottom of the ship and slept three bunks high. In the cramped quarters, I tossed and turned and managed to doze off to sleep. Then a sudden, piercing alarm shook me out of my slumber.

"This is not a drill, repeat, this is not a drill," blared the voice on the ship's loudspeaker.

"All hands on deck!"

"Everybody! Get topside with all your gear! This is not a drill!"

I scrambled off my bunk and rushed topside into the night. It was pitch dark. I looked to the horizon and saw ships . . . a flotilla, an entire fleet. There were so many ships.

I still didn't know where we were. I saw nets dangling over the railing of the ship. If we were getting ready to disembark and attack, this is what we had trained for. I waited for the next order. I was scared, but my adrenaline kicked in. I visualized throwing myself over the railing, climbing down via the nets, then jumping into the small Papa landing crafts. If we hit the ground, I would engage the enemy.

As quickly as it began, though, it ended.

"Return to your quarters," I heard over the loudspeaker.

Sighing with relief, I returned to my bunk for another sleepless night. Many, many years later, I pieced together my part of those thirteen days in October when the world was on the brink of nuclear war.

We were the fighting force on tap to invade Cuba, if necessary, in response to the Cuban Missile Crisis. President Kennedy knew the Soviet Union and Cuba had placed nuclear missile sites on Cuba and within striking distance of the US homeland. The president decided to place a ring of ships as a naval blockade around Cuba. He demanded the removal of the missiles already there and the destruction of the sites. It was a showdown between super-powers, and I was in the middle of it.

The stakes were high as the world held its breath. Under the specter of Mutually Assured Destruction, the leaders of both super-powers grappled with the possibility of a catastrophic nuclear war. The US and Soviet Union made a deal. The Soviets dismantled the weapon sites in exchange for a pledge from the US not to invade Cuba. The Cuban Missile Crisis was over, and thankfully we never had to hit the beaches.

Several months later, I was officially assigned to Guantanamo Bay (or GTMO, pronounced "Git-mo"), Cuba. I was in charge of communications, laying communications cable from the leeward side to the windward side of Cuba. I was there for three months with 1,500 Marines. The Corps had a policy of rotating Marines out every three months. In a short time, we really got to know each other and formed strong friendships at GTMO. No matter what the policy, we had a common bond to stand guard and protect American interests.

Fidel Castro's Cuban soldiers looked down on our guys from a higher ridgeline and through the barrels of Cuban tanks. The days and nights of my fellow Marines were usually spent dug in along the fence line (barbed wire) that separated us from the Cuban soldiers. The US Navy's 7th Fleet was in the bay and covered our backs. If hostilities broke out, our commanding officer told us we were expendable and that our life expectancy was a mere few minutes. Recreation and relaxation were welcome diversions from the grim reality that you could die in seconds.

For recreation, I got creative and built an outdoor cinema. I had my communications team string up several sheets on poles to make a screen for evening movie shows.

I sold hot dogs, popcorn, and soda and showed some great movies, courtesy of the US Navy. The Marines came to the cinema and relaxed. They loved it. I felt that I was helping them get through the three-month tour. I used the money to build a new mess hall. In those three months, I gained a reputation for spinning up projects no one else would dare to. I leaned forward and found ways to turn things around.

Even the Cubans who were cleared to work at GTMO loved me. My parents were Cuban, and I spoke Spanish. Somewhere on that island, the Garcia family had owned a tobacco plantation before the revolution. The Cubans felt comfortable and safe with me. We talked about Cuban life and what the people were going through. They brought me Cuban sandwiches, which was a special treat.

"How did you get those sandwiches, Garcia?" my buddies asked.

"I'm Cuban," I smiled charismatically. In this respect, I was just like my Dad—a charmer.

Okinawa, Japan

After my three months at GTMO, I went back to Camp Lejeune, and then to Okinawa, The Rock. I was on The Rock for thirteen months. Okinawa, south of Japan, is part of the Ryukyu archipelago. We exercised and employed training maneuvers in places like the Philippines, Japan, and Taiwan for six months. Our floating battalion landing team (BLT) practiced and disembarked from the boats, onto nets, and into Papa boats. The waters were choppy, and we had to get into the boats without being crushed, slammed, or thrown into those rough waters. We practiced and perfected amphibious beach landings.

One night, coming back from liberty (an authorized pass), I returned to the barracks after partying with friends. I tried to enter the barracks quietly and get into bed without waking anyone in the squad bay. The only light came from the latrine, and it dimly lit the squad area. As I approached my bunk, I saw the silhouette of my friend sitting on a footlocker at the base of my bunk. He was hunched over, elbows on his knees, his face buried in his hands.

I heard him crying. Marines don't cry. I asked myself, "Why is he crying?"

I put my hand on his shoulder and asked, "Are you ok? What happened?"

My friend looked up at me and said quietly, "Don't you know?"

"Know what?"

"President Kennedy was killed."

Time stopped on November 22, 1963. There were no words.

We were far away from home, and all were shocked in disbelief and grief. Lee Harvey Oswald had fatally shot John F. Kennedy while the president was traveling in a motorcade with his wife, Jacqueline. Our president was assassinated. That night in the barracks, it was quiet enough to hear a pin drop. Only our sobs broke the silence. As the news spread, many of us stood in lines to use the telephones. We reached out to loved ones to comfort and to be comforted. I heard some of them.

"Can you believe it?"

"How are you doing?"

"Are you OK?"

"I love you."

This was a moment I would never forget. Our commander in chief was dead. I remembered exactly where I was and how I felt when I heard the news. I was emotionally drained, sapped. It felt like another low blow, and I pulled myself together.

"What's next?" I thought.

My Marine Corps training and discipline prepared me to stay focused and deal with all situations, including this one. The physical and psychological training prepared me to know my enemy and how to defeat him.

The Marine Corps grounded me; it taught me to be fearless and to face danger head-on. I watched the movie *The DI* (with Jack Webb). Details of the barracks, the DIs, the training, and the brotherhood were realistic and accurate. This movie brought back good memories and reinforced that Marines do what must be done in life.

After I finished my tour in Okinawa, I went back to the states for a few weeks of leave to see my family and friends. I needed all the discipline, strength, and poise as I prepared to return home to New York City, the concrete jungle, and start a family.

CHAPTER 3:

Peace, Love, and Music

After leaving Okinawa and dealing with the gnawing sense of loss from the passing of President Kennedy, I thought I was ready to start my family. I thought I'd be a good husband to my high school sweetheart back in Brooklyn, and a good father.

When I returned to Brooklyn, the people in the neighborhood welcomed me. They liked and respected me, and even looked up to me.

They said, "Danny, you look so handsome and fit in your uniform."

In Brooklyn, I proposed to Lola, and she accepted. The year was 1966.

I returned to Hollis, Queens, to the home of my Titi Red and Uncle Victor. I was like a son to them. As their gift to me, they paid for the entire wedding. On the day of the wedding, as I was putting on my uniform, my Uncle Victor came up into my attic room and talked to me like a father.

"Are you sure this is what you want to do?" Uncle Victor asked.

"Yes," I replied. I looked him in the face as a man ready to be married.

Uncle Victor simply nodded, turned away, and went back downstairs.

On January 15, 1966, in the splendor of a full military story-book wedding, we married. The wedding and reception were just like the movie *The Deer Hunter* with Robert De Niro.

Our first home was in Williamsburg, Brooklyn; a two-story brown, stone apartment on the second floor. Her sister lived across the street, and her mother was about five blocks away. Lola was close to her mother and sisters. We were young and happy to be together.

Our first son arrived on January 2, 1967.

Before long, I was ordered to the Marine barracks at Naval Air Station Corpus Christi, Texas. I packed my bags and moved with my family. During the two years that we lived in Texas, I worked in the military prison as a brig supervisor. We welcomed our daughter a year after we arrived (January 1968).

"We Didn't Issue You a Wife"

In Corpus Christi, Texas, we lived in military housing on the base. I was away from morning to night performing brig duties, then exercising military tactics sometimes six or seven days a week. Our priority as Marines was to be ready to deploy and fight at a moment's notice. My wife, like other military wives, was left to create a life raising infants.

The Marines had a saying: "We issued you a sea bag; we didn't issue you a wife." The wives and families had to understand and accept the long absences from home. The strain of military life often breaks families, as I soon experienced. My wife was homesick for her family in New York.

One by one, my brother Marines in my unit were pulled and assigned to support the Vietnam War. Few came back alive. During this time, my commanding officer told the unit that my dear friend Sgt Eaglin had been injured and died two days from port while on a hospital ship. I was the best man in his wedding. Staff Sergeant Patton, who was our judo instructor, deployed twice. On the second tour in Vietnam, he was killed in action. I was part of the honor guard burial detail and laid many of my fellow Marines to rest. Witnessing their departures and then having to bury them . . . it tore at me. I couldn't bear any more of my friends dying and having to bury another Marine brother.

I decided to make a change—to leave the Marine Corps. I sent my wife and children back to Brooklyn, New York. I stayed in Texas.

After being discharged from the Marine Corps in Corpus Christi, I enlisted in the US Air Force. In San Antonio, Texas, I lived by myself and attended Cryptology School. After several months, the Air Force canceled the course because they discovered a Russian spy in the class. My short time in the Air Force was over, and I returned to Brooklyn to be with my wife and kids.

That's when I started working for Shell Oil Company in New York City (1968–69) and in Houston, Texas (1970–72). My third child, a girl, was born in New York in December 1968. My youngest son was also born in New York in 1970.

Shell Oil Company

Following my experience with the Air Force, I was still young, aggressive, and eager to learn. I sent out resumes, and one of those I sent to Shell Oil in the RCA Building in New York City. After several interviews, Shell Oil offered me a job in their transportation and supply department.

My job was to code. I had no idea what coding was. Soon, I learned that coding is transforming data from numbers and putting them onto a sheet of paper that goes into a computer. Coding is related to keypunch operations like what my mother and aunt had done for IBM. I couldn't believe that's all I had to do. Later, I took the information and transferred it to a chart for presentation. I didn't know what the charts were for, but I used my colored pencils and, with a bit of creativity, livened up the presentations. The graphic charts I created were excellent because, in one year, I received three merit raises.

During the 1970s, businesses began to support and provide equal employment opportunity (EEO) for minorities. I was a proven performer and considered a racial minority (Hispanic).

"You know, there is a position opening up in public relations," my boss told me. "They are looking for a minority. We'd like to see you in the position. Are you interested?"

I replied, "OK, let's keep talking."

He went on to state that they wanted to meet me and gave me more information on the position

My work with the chart presentations impressed Shell Oil's art director. When I interviewed with him, he liked me immediately. He noticed my passion and charisma and offered me the job. I accepted the position and found myself working for Shell on the 50th floor of the RCA building. From my new office, I could look down and watch the Rockettes practicing at Radio City Music Hall. I felt like I was on top of the world.

The head of our department said, "Are you aware the charts and graphs you work on are going to the president of Shell? Do you know that he is taking them to London and presenting them to the president of Royal Dutch, who owns 66 percent of Shell shares?"

I had no idea. I just knew that I enjoyed what I was doing and was improving more and more.

"Is there anything you need to make the charts better?" the executive queried.

"Well," I pondered, "I could use some different color tape strips and designs to make the charts stand out." Shell provided me with everything I needed to create and produce those graphic charts. Shell continued to finance whatever I needed to do my job, and my charts continued to be presented to executives in England.

My Executive Mentor, Bud Roberts

Any success I achieved while with Shell Oil was because of my art director and mentor, Bud Roberts. Bud was a legend, a hero within Shell, and one of Shell's first Key Club members. When I met him, he had been with Shell for over forty-five years. There was nothing he couldn't do or make happen. He ran the entire public relations department, which developed branding images such as the Shell logo, recognized all over the world. He conceived and published over 2,000 educational materials for schools and created *Shell's Wonderful World of Golf* TV production and the *Shell Diary*.

Bud noticed my creativity and willingness to work long hours seven days a week. Bud was a workaholic, and together we established a father-and-son type of relationship. We collaborated on

Shell's public relations projects. Bud mentored me and became like a father to me.

"I want you to learn about everything I do," Bud mused as he walked me into a huge room, an expansive repository.

"I want you to know and work in every facet of public relations. In fact, you're going to be in charge of the Shell library."

The task was daunting. The Shell library housed hundreds of thousands of negatives and transparencies stored in row after row of file cabinets. The library contained information about Shell Oil and its history from annual reports to myriads of promotional pictures taken by Shell's professional photographers, such as Forrest Adrian. (A glimpse of the photo library in *The Secret Life of Walter Mitty*, starring Ben Stiller, illustrates the vastness of the Shell library's material)

Bud gave me the task of managing the file system of the vast library and its contents. I put in the work and hours to achieve excellence. I enjoyed working in the film library, learning about Shell Oil Company. Bud opened the door for me to work with top-notch photographers hired to shoot in remote and tropical locations. Their photographs were used in a dye-transfer process which made the pictures jump right off the pages of the *Shell Diary*. Bud created the Shell Diary as a promotional piece. It contained colorful dye-transfer prints of underwater photography from exotic locations. The photos of underwater life and shells were stunning. The best international professional photographers worked with us.

From production layout to distribution, I learned it all. People from other countries worked alongside me. We were a team. I found my new family at Shell Oil Company and with Bud Roberts.

Bud and I socialized outside of work as well. We went to the Red Baron restaurant for dinner and drinks. We talked about business, creative ideas, and my future at Shell. I loved it.

"Danny, I envision you succeeding me," he once told me.

I was excited about the prospects. I continued to absorb the knowledge of the inner workings of public relations for an international enterprise and all that it entailed. I knew Bud was proud of me.

Bud was from England and was very proper and polished. He always dressed to a *T*. He modeled his sophistication for me and taught me how to present myself as a gentleman and a businessman. Bud taught me how to tie a tie, how to cross my legs, and how to wear a suit. A proper gentleman—that's what he wanted me to become, and I was up for it. In New York City, as in the Marine Corps, my charismatic personality continued to draw people to me, and I enjoyed interacting with them.

Bud had a German girlfriend, Renati, who was a great artiste. Together, they were my corporate parents, cultivating me, molding me, guiding me. They talked to me and educated me in the very proper English style. Bud and Renati never gave up on me.

Because I was so outgoing, it seemed like everyone in the Shell building knew me. Bud said to Renati, "How does this kid do it? Everyone knows who he is!"

"Hey, kid, put these letters on your phone," Bud once told me.

"What letters?"

"Ready?" he asked. "T-H-I-N-K. When you start talking on that phone, you read those words and think first before you talk." In that one simple lesson, he taught me how to not react impulsively, to pause, and to think before opening my mouth. That was an ongoing lesson in my time with Bud, one which he shares with the entire corporation.

He went on: "We're doing a poster with you." Bud had a PR message for the corporation, and I was to be the model.

"What? What kind of poster?" I was puzzled, but before I could speak, Bud attempted to put a piece of duct tape over my mouth. I shook my head back and forth and protested, "I don't think so!"

Of course, I could have refused, yet Bud won. The photographer took the photo, and the art department created a poster. They airbrushed the word "CONFIDENTIALITY" over the picture of me with tape over my mouth. Shell sent that poster all over the world. Thanks to Bud and his genius, I became well-known in Shell Oil (yes, as a "poster" child) and established an enduring and adventurous relationship with Bud and Shell.

Promoting Woodstock, the Concert

During my time with Shell Oil in Manhattan, New York, a home-grown concert nearby exploded into a major historical event in August 1969: Woodstock. The Woodstock festival stood for peace, love, and masses of young people. The Woodstock Music & Art Fair was a three-day musical festival on a six-hundred-acre dairy farm in the Catskills (Bethel, New York), and was a pivotal event in American music. Many considered it the greatest musical happening of all time.

I was part of Woodstock history as one of the promoters and as an attendee. It started when a friend of mine came to visit me in my office on the 50th floor of the RCA building.

"Danny, I need your help," said my friend. "I know you're working here at Shell and you're in PR. I'm helping a friend who's doing a concert at Woodstock with a bunch of local artists coming. We're selling tickets, and I think it will be fun."

We talked a little bit, and he showed me the tickets. My friend wanted me to help promote the concert. There were many other volunteers who gave time and finances too.

I agreed and said, "Well, OK, I'll see what I can do. I'll make some phone calls."

As a promoter, I used every public relations vehicle at my disposal to get the word out about the concert. I talked to many people and told them to contact my friend for details and tickets. The main concert organizer had already contacted the media. News spread about Woodstock by word of mouth as well.

During the Vietnam War era, the US government initiated a draft of young people into military service to support the war. The youths protested, some did not want to go. Woodstock was a platform of expression to declare, "Stop the war! Power to the people! Peace, not war!"

I heard that ticket sales for Woodstock topped over 100,000 prior to the festival's opening weekend! My good friend asked me to go to the concert, and I agreed. I was curious.

I asked myself, "What would it be like to attend an outdoor concert with people from all over the country . . . all over the world?" I wanted to be part of it, helping in any way I could like so many others.

The day I left from the Port Authority bus terminal in New York City, young people had jammed the place waiting for buses. There was a girl standing on the shoulders of a guy in the middle of this huge crowd. Over her head she raised a cigarette lighter in her hand, waving and flicking the lighter switch. With the flame, she tried to activate the sprinkler system at Port Authority.

The crowd cheered, "Yes! You can do it! Just a little higher, over to the left." They encouraged the balancing duo to keep trying to get the sprinklers to go off.

Meanwhile, the police fought their way through the crowd to get to the girl. Just as the police got close to her, the sprinkler system triggered. The wet crowd cheered. On that note, I turned and moved toward my bus.

The bus approached the dairy farm in Bethel, New York, and it was pitch dark. There was one road in and one road out. As my bus came over the top of a hill, I looked down and saw cars lined up bumper to bumper, their lights extending down the hill and beyond sight. Those of us who were part of the 60,000 early attendees clogged the roads to Woodstock in August of 1969. The dairy farm was not designed for the arrival of hundreds of thousands of people. A girl on our bus became frightened and lost it.

She screamed, "I want to go home!"

It was obvious there was no turning back and no quick exit.

As we proceeded to exit the bus, a guy approached me saying, "Hey, can I talk to you for a moment?"

"OK."

He opened an attaché case filled with drugs of every type arranged in orderly, neat little packages.

"I have everything you need to get high," he boasted. This was my introduction to Woodstock.

"No thanks," I declined. I wasn't there for the drugs. I was there for the music and the experience.

I stepped off the bus and walked into the open, flat field where people were sleeping out in the open. Like everyone else, I slept in that open field with a blanket, and in the mud. It was cold and wet because it rained every day I was there. The next morning, the nearby pond (Filippini Pond) filled with people bathing, laughing, and singing.

I recognized a big contrast between being in the Marine Corps, serving my country and fighting, and participating in what Woodstock represented: getting high, peace, drugs, and music. The Woodstock vibe was different from anything I ever experienced.

Woodstock was a concert for peace; a love-fest of people of different colors, languages, and cultures. Music was the instrument to bring people together in harmony. I stayed to the end, eager to learn something new. I was amazed that so many people could gather for peace and, in the midst, be peaceful themselves.

On the first day of the concert, people tore down the fences. At that point, Woodstock became a free concert. Who could stop them? There were too many people arriving in droves. While all this was going on, the media reported the growing magnitude of the crowd: nearly 400,000. The enormous crowds drew some of the most well-known performers of the time, such as Janis Joplin; Santana; the Grateful Dead; Jimi Hendrix; Jefferson Airplane; and Crosby, Stills, Nash & Young. Woodstock evolved into a phenomenon.

The voice over the loudspeaker periodically announced calls for people needing medical assistance. Concertgoers were under the influence of drugs of all kinds, and they needed medical help. One guy who was high climbed up on the rafter by the stage lights, fell off, and ended up going to the hospital. Another time, a helicopter flew in and picked up a pregnant woman who was about to deliver.

The massive concert crowd totally outnumbered and overwhelmed the police. Rather than arresting people, the police eventually walked through the crowds, facilitating and assisting people who needed help or directions. Still more people continued to come.

Personally, I was caught up in the music. I soaked in the creativity of every performance, every instrument. As the artists played, I sang with the people. We enjoyed the professional musicians, different artists every day, and it was free. A concert like Woodstock had never been done before.

More than a home-grown concert, Woodstock became a happening. The connection between people was amazing. Music, unity, and peace touched people—even those who did not attend in person. It was a musical extravaganza. Woodstock, as a cultural event, illustrated that people can come together in peace, not hurting each other, but helping each other. Woodstock was social harmony, traffic jams, cooperation, and generosity amongst good-natured people.

The last announcement I heard as I was leaving the concert was "Be sure to see your doctor and get checked out. There's an epidemic of hepatitis."

I was glad I chose to stay. The music was great, and the people were great. Although the rains muddied the fields and roads, the people endured the bad weather and the mud to be part of history.

My art director, Bud Roberts, asked me, "Where were you? Where did you go?"

"I went to Woodstock."

"Woodstock? You were at Woodstock?" By the look on his face, he, too, was amazed that I was there, but said no more. He had something else on his mind, something work-related.

Back to The Lone Star State: Texas

In the 1970s, Shell Oil planned its future and diversification and decided to move its corporate headquarters.

Bud told me, "Danny, we're going to be moving. Shell is moving to Houston, Texas. I need you to be a part of that move and come with me."

"Are you kidding? I don't want to go to Houston. I don't ride horses. I'm not a cowboy. I'm a city boy from New York," I chuckled.

After a fatherly pause, Bud said, "Go there, stay for a few weeks, check it out. I need you to help me set up the PR department." Bud also wanted me in Houston as his right-hand man.

I flew to Texas, the Lone Star State, and landed in Houston. I stayed at the Marriott and started to get familiar with the people and the environment. Our team began to replicate the various departments of Shell's public relations operations in New York City. I continued my work with Shell's annual report, the Shell logo, Shell library, and the *Shell Diary*.

At night, I relaxed and visited restaurants and nightclubs. Houston was not a sprawling metropolis at the time, but Market Square seemed interesting. Market Square catered to the posh crowd, with buildings converted to house restaurants, classical music and jazz clubs, and the Magnolia Ballroom. I was intrigued. After a few weeks of discovering Houston, I decided to stay and work with Bud for a while. We moved into the new Shell Oil headquarters at 1 Shell Plaza.

Bud continued to commute back and forth to New York while I agreed to stay in Houston. Bud was ecstatic and assured me I would grow accustomed to the pace and lifestyle in Texas. He was incredibly focused and had a tremendous amount of responsibility as Shell Oil's art director. I was young and carefree and enjoyed interacting with people. As usual, we worked together, and I supported the business of the PR department. I also helped him to relax and enjoy himself in a social setting. For example, we ate at the classy Red Baron, with velvet wall coverings and plush carpets. The establishment's mascot greeted us. His name was Sparky, a spry dalmatian who loved to chew on ice. Before dinner, and drinking our cocktails, we fed Sparky his ice cubes. At the Red Baron, Bud, the fine English gentleman, felt at ease.

Night Life and Jazz

As a New Yorker, I was accustomed to action and the fast-paced life of the city that never sleeps. I found the Houston lifestyle too slow. I missed the liveliness and nightlife of New York. I missed the great music that surrounded me as a child. I found a club called La Bastille, which had a cellar-restaurant atmosphere and ran so deep underground it passed for a Parisian prison. In the 1970s, the club hosted jazz greats such as Dizzie Gillespie, Sarah Vaughan, Les McCann (featured in the documentary film *Soul to Soul*), Woody Herman, Yusef Lateef, and others. At other times, the club featured stand-up comedian acts such as Johnny Carson and Jackie Mason.

La Bastille was my kind of place, where I enjoyed music and cocktails and mingled with the staff and other guests. It wasn't long before the club considered me a regular. I felt right at home. I was natural and charismatic, and this attracted people to me. One night, the owners of La Bastille, "Fat Ernie" Criezis and his wife, Toni Renee, (both from New York) approached me and introduced themselves. Fat Ernie was your typical large, cigar-smoking, fast-talking promoter from New York. Toni was a cabaret singer; a nice-looking lady, quick to read and see through people. Toni handled the books and made sure the i's were dotted and the t's crossed. They lived in the fast lane and flew to New York and Europe looking for new talent. They were always looking to get the heads-up on a great opportunity. That night, I was the opportunity.

"Danny, you're always here," said Fat Ernie. "I know you work at Shell, but think about this. I'd like you to kind of, you know, 'manage' the place."

"You're kidding," I said with a grin. "Thanks, but I just come here to enjoy the music and take a step back from time to time."

Fat Ernie leaned forward and insisted, "I just want you to come, hang out with the people. Make sure the artists go on, on time. Just come and keep an eye on the place."

I agreed to try it, managing La Bastille. I did not need the money (Shell took very good care of me). What I needed was cultural and musical stimulation. After a day's work at Shell, I worked with Toni and Ernie at night. I already knew how to work with people and how to interact with musical artists. Each artist always wanted something special, so I accommodated them and made sure their needs were met.

Mongo Santamaría, for example, was a Cuban percussionist who played with my father. His Latin version of the pop single "Watermelon Man" was inducted into the Grammy Hall of Fame. He was well-known and played congas. My father knew Mongo because they played the same instruments and traveled in the same circles. Mongo always wanted fresh watermelon, so I made sure he had his fruit while he played at La Bastille. The club and the jazz music made me reminisce about my New York roots. For me, being at La Bastille felt like being in New York City and being at home.

After a few years in Houston, I experienced an internal pull, which told me there was more to life than what Houston had to offer. I observed that Bud spent more time in Houston, settling into Shell Oil's new headquarters. He still periodically went back to New York to work on the Shell logo and the *Shell Diary* and to complete the corporate move to Houston.

Even though I enjoyed my life, my work, and all the perks I had, I missed my children. No projects, activities, or people could replace them. Bud wished for us to continue working together in Houston, but I knew it was time for me to go. Houston was not New York; Houston was not home. I had to get back to my children.

When I decided to leave Shell Oil, I also left my dear friend and mentor, Bud Roberts. I left La Bastille and my life and job in Houston to return to New York.

Leaving Bud was a difficult decision. I was like the son he longed for, and he was to me the father I longed for. Bud wanted to pass his mantle to me, to pass on his lifelong knowledge of his Shell Oil work to me, his heir apparent. Nobody came close to dynamically managing his vast responsibilities, and he taught me how to do it all. It hurt me deeply when I left Bud.

Back in New York City, I briefly reunited with my children. Then I reenlisted in the Marine Corps. The Marine Corps was my military family. I missed my brothers in arms and the camaraderie we shared. It was 1972, the height of the Vietnam War, and I was sent to Southeast Asia, the Vietnam theater of operations.

CHAPTER 4:

Return to the Corps and Human Relations Fame

I wanted to be a part of the action of the Vietnam War. I missed what the Marine Corps stood for: structure, training, discipline, loyalty, and brotherhood. My Marine Corps family welcomed me back into the fold when I reenlisted. My previous years with Bud Roberts, when he groomed me to become a Shell Oil corporate executive, prepared me. When I returned to the Corps, I was more mature and polished as a leader.

Nam Phong, Thailand

From 1972–1973, I was stationed at Royal Thai Air Base Nam Phong, Thailand. In June 1972, Nam Phong became the main hub in theater for the USMC's 1st Marine Aircraft Wing, which flew air operations against targets in Vietnam, Cambodia, and Laos. We were constantly vigilant against the enemy.

During my first enlistment with the Marine Corps, my military occupational specialty (MOS) was communications specialist. The Marine Corps also trained me to go behind enemy lines as a forward observer, if necessary. But when I arrived in Thailand, my unit redirected me to another battle, within the ranks. The day I arrived, I went to the mess hall to eat. I got my tray of chow and sat in the middle of the mess hall. As I started to eat, I looked to my left toward the entrance of the mess hall and saw a couple of young Black Marines in uniform. They raced toward the chow line and the men standing, holding their trays and waiting for their food. As they ran behind the men, the Black Marines slashed several of the white Marines in the back of the neck with razor blades. The Black Marines ran out of the exit of the mess hall, and other Marines immediately responded to the bleeding men to help them.

I was shocked. What was happening?

When I reported to my commanding officer (CO), his orders were clear. "You've got to stop the drugs and racial problems, now! You're going to teach human relations. You're going to hold week-long classes for everyone starting right now. Here's the book."

The CO threw volume one of a book on human relations into my hands, and I caught the thick book. My new job was to teach human relations and stop drug and alcohol problems, but I did not know what the CO was talking about. I discovered that the human relations volumes were required reading for every Marine, with completion noted in each Marine's performance report or fitness report (FITREP). If a Marine didn't attend the classes, he was not eligible for the next promotion. It was mandatory training.

The Corps was aware of racial problems between the troops. Some Marines used racial slurs and hateful words toward each other (i.e., nigger, white trash, and spick). Often, the hostility between people of color and whites created situations of violence and anger within the ranks, such as the neck-slashing incident I witnessed. There was no room for any of this in the Corps. This racial divide tore down unit cohesion and the ability of Marines to fight as a team. I was told, in no uncertain terms, that it was my job to stop it. But how do you stop it?

I relied on everything I learned in the streets, my people skills, and communication tact to succeed. The Marines had implemented human relations classroom teaching as the means to stop racial problems: talk about it in the classroom for eight hours a day with about twenty guys. I had no formal experience with human relations, but I knew how to talk to people with respect and how to get their attention. In the beginning, the guys didn't want to go to the class. By day three of my class, they didn't want to leave.

I told my students, "I know you don't want to be here. I know you were forced to be in this class. However, we are going to have an opportunity to listen to each other without interrupting. Human relations is not a Black and white issue. It is about relationships with people."

Human relations was natural to me. Like in the streets of New York, I saw the root of racial tensions, and it wasn't just an issue of color. It was an issue of respect and people choosing to get along with one another for the common good. I saw such cooperation in Hell's Kitchen and at Woodstock—it was possible. I taught that someone from the South, for example, may not know how to relate to a person from New York (and vice versa). Based on one's cultural background and upbringing, a Marine could unknowingly say something hurtful and not be aware of it. I explained that people listen to what other people say and mimic those words, not knowing how those words hurt others. There were cases, though, where people were quite aware that their language, tone, and mannerisms were offensive. These people did not care. It was my job to help them to see the light. I introduced a different style of communicating, one which stopped the destructive racial and ethnic clashes which tore apart the teamwork and values of the Corps.

In the classroom, I told them plainly that words hurt. I started from ground zero, teaching Marines how to speak and listen respectfully to each other. I taught basic human interaction. Labels were damaging and unacceptable in the Corps.

Every day for the entire time I was there, I also worked with Marines who had problems with drugs and alcohol. Personally, I felt like I fought several battles at the same time. The war was raging in my own backyard within the ranks of my Marine Corps brothers. Right in front of me, my buddies were caught up in the drug culture, using speed to stay awake because they were on duty for long hours. I read body language and knew if someone was high. If someone used marijuana, I smelled it on them. Other indicators of drug use were slurring of speech, being late on the job, absenteeism (not showing up at all), and diminished performance. It was a wake-up call for me to see the devastating effects of drugs and alcohol.

Unfortunately, too many of my comrades were hooked. Drugs and alcohol were inexpensive and easily accessible. The Vietnamese were all too willing to supply drugs. Drugs and alcohol were coping mechanisms. They dulled or took away painful and horrific war memories, but the relief was momentary. Once the drugs wore off, the user found themselves in the same place. My brothers smoked drugs laced with morphine, amphetamines, and barbiturates. They drowned themselves in alcohol. They were hurting and needed help. The strong and mentally focused person refused and said no, choosing not to indulge. I was there to counsel them as best as I could.

The Corps had a program called Golden Flow, a daily urinalysis testing for drugs. One of my other jobs was to be a monitor for the program. Every month, I had the responsibility of collecting samples from 3,000 Marines. I had to label every sample and forward it to the testing site. If a Marine's sample tested positive, he did not fly out of theater and could not reenter the states. The Marine was confined and treated.

One day, I had an officer come through when I was on Golden Flow duty. It was his turn, but he would have nothing of it.

"Sir, here's your bottle, please provide a specimen," I instructed.

His curt reply was "I'm not peeing in the bottle."

I said again, "Sir, everyone needs to pee in the bottle." Again, the officer refused.

"OK, sir," I said respectfully.

It was not my drug testing program. I was just a Marine responsible for implementing it on behalf of the CO. I took the empty bottle to my CO and let him know what happened. The next day, I saw the same officer peeing in the bottle.

My reputation grew and preceded me back in the United States. Major Charles Krulak, the son of Lt General Victor "Brute" Krulak was looking for immediate help on his base in California.

"I'm having problems in North Island, Coronado. I need somebody who's cross-trained in human relations, drugs, et cetera, et cetera, to come to Coronado," said the Major. I had the qualifications he needed and was hand-picked for the job in California—a dream job. The timing was perfect.

Losing My Family

It was 1974. I completed my assignment in Thailand and left the Vietnam theater to go home for a few weeks of leave. I missed my family and was eager to see my wife and children.

I came home to Brooklyn and had high expectations about reviving my marriage. I had a great follow-on assignment lined up: shore duty working a nine-to-five job teaching human relations in San Diego, California. It was a plush assignment. I thought my wife would be as excited as I was to be going to the land of sunshine.

"We're going to San Diego, California," I announced with much enthusiasm.

I envisioned more time with my kids and beginning to have a real family life. For several days, I raved about how great California would be. Eventually, though, I noticed that my wife was not responding, not communicating. She was passive and silent.

She said quietly, "I really don't want to go. The kids and I are settled here. I don't think we should go; I think it best that we stay. I don't want to move."

I was in disbelief. This was a travel opportunity for her and the kids to go to the West Coast, a chance to experience beaches, surfing, and all that California had to offer.

Toward the end of my leave, while I was still in Brooklyn, she took the kids to a babysitter. When I went to pick up the kids, I was surprised to see my wife coming out of a car with two men in suits. I was in my USMC uniform, a Sergeant at the time.

The men in suits approached me and said, "Sergeant, can we speak to you in the hallway?"

"Who are these people?" I thought to myself, mystified. "What's going on?"

My wife said nothing and disappeared into the building like a shadow.

"We're detectives," the men replied and identified themselves. They showed me their badges and continued, "We would like to talk with you in the hallway."

The men escorted me into the building, pausing to compose themselves before they delivered me a crushing blow. The detectives told me, "Your wife does not love you and does not want be with you anymore. She does not want to go to California with you."

They were the living, breathing essence of a classic Dear John letter, delivered in person.

I felt like they had stabbed me in the chest. I was shocked and devastated. The words I heard felt like a blazing knife ripping through me and laying my heart bare and vulnerable. I pulled myself together with all the strength I had.

"What about my kids?" I asked. "My kids are upstairs. I'm going up to see my kids, and nobody's going to stop me." I felt the street rise in me, ready to fight if I needed to.

"Sergeant, we understand, but you *don't* want to do this," the detectives advised.

"If you try to go upstairs, we will stop you," they warned.

They stood shoulder to shoulder and positioned themselves between me and the stairs to the apartment. Although they were sympathetic, they had a job to do. They were there to keep me from bolting upstairs to see my kids. There was no court order, just two detectives in suits who blocked my passage and made sure I did not go into the babysitter's home that day.

"She's afraid. She doesn't want to go with you. She is just afraid of you," explained the detectives.

I got the message loud and clear. My wife closed the door and put me out; out of the picture, out of their lives. She made her choice, and I had no choice but to accept it.

Rather than make a scene or fight the detectives, I turned and walked away. I wasn't allowed to hold my children one last time or even say goodbye. Reasoning with myself, I decided it was better for me to leave and not make trouble. I just left. I had my orders to San Diego, so that's where I went.

Being forced to walk away and leave my kids in that Brooklyn apartment was one of the most excruciating times in my life. It felt like a death sentence; I had no breath. As I walked away, I recalled the times when my children played ball with their cousins in the park, laughing and running toward the jingle of the ice-cream bell. I pictured myself turning my pockets inside out for loose change so they could buy the treat of the day.

I knew I couldn't take my children with me. I was in the Marines. The concept of a single father was not common, and it certainly wasn't acceptable for a Marine. There was no way to make it work.

I lost my family; I failed. I never lost, so I wasn't accustomed to losing. I *always* won, so, truly, I was in a state of shock.

The pieces came together a few years later. I recollected another time when I had returned from overseas. She was supposed to pick me up at the airport in a brand-new car I had bought for her and had shipped from overseas. My brother-in-law told me she had gotten into an accident on the way. She wasn't hurt, so my brother-in-law told me to come to his apartment in Brooklyn. My kids were there, and we were playing. My first son was maybe seven years old at the time.

"We had another daddy while you were gone," said my son.

I did not react or respond outwardly. My wife explained away the other daddy by saying he was just a friend and that she was just doing his laundry. This confirmed that she found someone else when I was away from home and serving my country overseas.

My Truth, My Reality

I wrote this portion of the book to tell *my truth* from *my perspective*. I was a Marine returning from the Vietnam War, where I constantly dealt with issues of life and death. No one told my children how and why I left them in Brooklyn. My children did not know that the two detectives blocked me from seeing them. I did not know how my children felt—if they even missed me. I knew for certain that separation from my children ripped my heart right out of me.

Honestly, most men don't talk much about feelings. Most men won't talk about their emotions at all. I was no different as a twenty-nine-year-old Marine. I recalled flipping through TV channels one night and finding a movie about a military man and his young wife. The story was so much like my own. The movie was about the man's loyalty to his brothers in arms and how he reenlisted to shoulder the burden of wartime deployment. The young soldier's wife couldn't understand how he chose the military over her and the family. Earlier in their marriage, she wrote him often about the details of home, tasks, her concerns, and deepest thoughts. After he reenlisted and left her again, she became distant and stopped writing. The weight of the separation and the loss of the relationship with his love was more than he could bear. His buddies received letters, and he became depressed because he had not heard from his wife.

And then the young man did receive a letter. A Dear John letter.

"I can't be with you, and I don't love you," wrote his wife.

The letter pierced the young soldier. He wanted to commit suicide.

I related to this story. I attempted to commit suicide by driving my car off the road. For years, I stuffed my emotions and tried to disguise my deep hurt from the world. I agonized over the loss of my family. God had to break me before he could bless me, and losing my family was one of those breaking times for me.

I was a great communicator, an extrovert who talked fast and entertained. I wrote to my family while I was in Thailand. Like the soldier in the movie, I did not receive letters in return; not a single letter or postcard while I was away at war. I hid my pain, longing to hear from home.

I didn't tell anyone my heart was broken. I remained stoic and silent.

Marines don't cry.

A voice in my head kept repeating, "She doesn't love you."

I felt rejection and isolation. I wanted to scream, shout, punch someone—anything to relieve the searing pain in my heart. My mother told me we were too young and shouldn't have gotten married. Like my father, I was away from home most of the time. I really did not know her, and she really did not know me.

I had to keep it together. Although I was broken, I did not show weakness and appeared confident when I was emotionally empty. Communication with family grew even more scarce, and I did not return to New York to visit. I decided I would not go to a place where I was no longer wanted.

I thought that when my kids got old enough we would find each other. After a ten-year separation, I divorced my first wife in 1982.

My firstborn son missed me the most and wanted to be with me in California. He longed to know his father, just as I longed to know my father, Jose "Bilingue" Garcia.

I believe God *allowed it all to happen* just the way it did. The betrayal, pain, and sorrow I felt gave me empathy for others. The loss helped me minister to others across the world who have felt some of the same dreadful feelings.

God allowed me to suffer, and then He equipped me to rely, not on myself, but on His Spirit of truth and counsel. Through this tragedy, I have helped others dig out of the divorce rut and live another day, another life.

Alone in North Island

Alone and without my family, I reported in March 1974 to the Marine Barracks at Naval Air Station North Island in San Diego, California. I was twenty-nine years old. I was to have three Command NCO jobs working in drug and alcohol abuse, career counseling, and human relations/leadership. After my success in the Vietnam theater with reducing racial tensions and drug use, I had gained notoriety and fame. It wasn't long before the command realized I didn't have any schooling in human relations and was flying by the seat of my pants.

"Garcia, you have to go to school," said Major Krulak, my commanding officer.

I would be going to school to be officially qualified and accredited as a Marine Corps human relations instructor. Admin cut me new orders to report to Marine Corps Recruit Depot in San Diego, also home of the Human Relations Institute. I reported late on a Friday and had nowhere to sleep. They put me in the empty squad bay, where I stayed over the weekend until I could be processed for school.

It must have been late at night; I was so numb. I could only put one foot in front of another to find my way to my quarters. I walked into a barrack with a long hallway. My duffel bag was draped over my shoulder. There was nobody there; all the bunks were empty. A single bare light dangling from the ceiling was all that lit the barrack. Staring at the light at the end of the hall was like being in the twilight zone, transported to another place and time.

I was completely alone in the quietness. Thoughts of rejection and betrayal lingered, but Marines don't cry. I tried to quiet my mind and reflect on what had happened to me: I returned from war, was confronted with a Dear John letter from my wife, and had my children stripped away from me. I felt dead.

I started class the following Monday with new quarters and my schedule of instruction at the Human Relations Institute. In the beginning, I didn't go out and only went to school. My Marine Corps buddies would check in on me because they were concerned, but I refused all social engagements. Sinking in despair was not my nature. I had to snap out of it. The instructors were persistent, though, and continually invited me to their homes for dinner and to meet their families. They spent many nights just listening to me. It was their concern for me and my welfare that snapped me out of my despair. Marines don't leave their wounded behind, and they carried me through the trauma of losing my family.

This phase lasted for three months while I was in school.

"Human Relations Makes Garcia's Day"

In the three-month course, accredited by Pepperdine University, I learned theory and concepts about human relations used in other parts of the world and adopted by the USMC. The Marine Corps used the techniques of Dr. Robert L. Humphrey to abolish anti-US sentiments in Europe. He was a decorated Marine and rifle platoon leader who survived the battle of Iwo Jima. His tools eliminated situations that interfered with and degraded mission accomplishment. His "win the people" methods were born out in Combined Action Platoons where US Marines lived with peasants and integrated with the locals. His "Life Values" principles worked—they successfully stopped the violence and promoted cross-cultural harmony.

I met Dr. Humphrey several times, and he shared his life's work with me. He taught the universal human moral values which promote peace and personal happiness and stop conflict, including cross-cultural conflict. Dr. Humphrey devised the formula: Self + Others = Dual Life Value. First, an individual's self-value is important. Secondly, one reaches their full potential and highest level of consciousness when one acknowledges the need for others.

I graduated from the class fully certified as a USMC human relations instructor. Reporting back to North Island in San Diego, I wasted no time. I immediately started teaching the mandatory human relations course to all ranks, from young privates to seasoned generals. As in Thailand, the Marines of North Island really did not want to sit in a human relations class taught by a Sergeant, me, who was junior in rank to most of them.

I told my students, "Human relations doesn't only mean relations between Black and white. It means cooperation between all people—Black, white, rich, blind, homeless, military, civilian . . . all people."

I adopted some unorthodox teaching practices. During the first few days, I assessed each student and figured out each person's weakness. If a person was prejudiced against the police, for instance, I sent him out riding around with the police department so he could see things from a police officer's perspective. One Marine worked at the Center for the Blind. I sent others to hospital wards. I sent one man to stay in a Tijuana jail for a few days with only the police and Marines knowing his identity.

I managed the three different command programs and made a name for myself. I requisitioned furniture and decorated my office like a corporate headquarters, like the office I had at Shell Oil in New York's RCA building. My office looked better than those of my superior officers. While I worked for Major Krulak, the first-term reenlistment rate for the command jumped 600 percent (from 7.6 percent to 47.1 percent), one of the highest reenlistment averages in the Marine Corps at the time. Statistics confirmed that drug use at North Island continued to steadily decrease. I had the support of the CO and, because I got results, no one of any rank challenged my training methods.

My unorthodox methods, coupled with the foundation of the Institute's theory, proved extremely effective. I searched for and found outlets for my creativity and high energy. I ran the human relations program and implemented action programs for the Marines in my classes. I focused on the troops with drug and alcohol problems and, through the human relations action programs, encouraged the Marines to reach out to the community. The North Islander newspaper published an article titled "Human Relations Makes Garcia's Day" and described the Marines who volunteered to work with children. Once, I threw a party for underprivileged children—their first real party—and the newspaper wrote about it. The CO said, "80 percent of the Marines on base were actively involved in several community outreach programs, and 100 percent of the Marines were involved in at least one program."

All my attention and energy were devoted to my work, 24-7. The racial incidents, the drug and alcohol problems, everything of a negative nature, ceased. In addition, within the command, the morale of the troops increased dramatically. Every individual who took the course wrote letters and critiques of the course. These letters validated and confirmed that what I taught them helped change their lives.

My time as a human relations instructor was a defining point in my life. To me, it was not just a course or techniques, it was a way of life. The Corps challenged me with a difficult task, but also prepared me for success through Dr. Humphrey's training methods and tools to stop violence and drug use. Students left my class with renewed respect for each other. By broadening their perspectives, they changed for the better and learned to care for and engage with the local community. I realized I loved to help people, and *I was good at it.*

Leadership Mentor, USMC Major Charles C. Krulak

My CO was an outstanding leader, a Vietnam combat veteran, and a man who led with integrity. I respected him. He supported and believed in me, and none of the successes I noted at North Island would have been possible without his OK and blessing. I considered Major Krulak my leadership mentor because he was discerning and measured the character of a man. He took the time to visit his troops, talk to them, and show his genuine concern. He cared for his troops. Steering them away from drugs and alcohol and teaching them to relate to each other made for Marine unit cohesion.

As my CO, he gave me an open-door policy. I could talk to him anytime about anything. He trusted me to execute the Human Relations Program, including the controversial training scenarios and backed me up in every way. Make no mistake, trusting an enlisted man to carry out such an important program was a risk. He trusted me, period. I implemented the program under his authority, and no one messed with or interfered with me. His leadership yielded extraordinary results in the lives of his Marines. As a leader, Major Krulak's actions were always focused on improving the lives and welfare of his men, which is why he is considered "a Marine's Marine." They would follow him anywhere.

As I came to the end of my enlistment in 1975, Major Krulak wrote and signed a Meritorious Mast, recognition for "the performance of an enlisted Marine . . . considered noteworthy or commendable beyond the usual requirements of duty or [when] the Marine demonstrates exceptional industry, judgment, or initiative." He summarized what I had done and commended my work as noteworthy.

I had to decide if I wanted to stay in the Corps or get out. I thought about the very same questions that I asked as a recruiter. Major Krulak called me into his office.

"Sgt Garcia, are you planning on staying in or getting out? You should stay in the Corps and go through the officer program. I would like you to be commissioned as an officer," said the Major. He knew how effective I was with everyone I met and wanted me to stay in.

It was a tempting offer from a man I admired.

"Major Krulak, I appreciate everything that you and the Corps have done for me. I love the Corps, and I love my country. However, I feel there is something out there that I am supposed to be doing. I won't know what it is until I leave."

I sensed he was a bit saddened, but he also recognized that I had a calling in my life outside of the Marine Corps. I decided to get out of the Corps and was honorably discharged.

I moved out of the Marine barracks on North Island and started living in Coronado. Because of the outreach action programs associated with the North Island Marines, the community knew me. Just like in my days at Shell Oil, I talked to people and networked. I made connections and nurtured relationships.

I stepped out on good footing and had to readjust to civilian life again.

CHAPTER 5:

Lost—Having It All, Having Nothing

In 1975, after leaving the Corps for a second time, I adjusted to civilian life by staying busy and engaged. The first job I took was for the Metropolitan Correction Center in San Diego, where I was a federal corrections officer. I also moved to a complex near San Diego State College. I was very social and loved to bring people together. I threw a party for college kids and people in my neighborhood. We partied. That's when I met my best friend, Curt, and many of his friends.

My Best Friend Curt

Curt was a tall, broad, dark Black man from Detroit. He was intelligent, a highly respected clinical psychologist. As soon as we met, we realized how much we had in common. We both came from the ghetto. We both loved music and concerts. We both worked with people who had drug addictions. We both loved to have fun and party.

Curt helped me to integrate back into civilian life. He invited me to move into his house with an indoor swimming pool, and we combined our resources. I furnished his house with pieces I brought back from Thailand. Curt and I were so close that we didn't have to talk because we knew what the other was thinking. I felt comfortable and stable with Curt.

We went to concerts such as Earth, Wind & Fire; Tower of Power; and Stevie Wonder. We took care of each other. With Curt's other friends, we formed a tight family of doctors, lawyers, nurses, and educators. Together, we knew a lot of influential people in San Diego.

I had it all, I thought. I had the things the world convinced me was a measure of success. As I became financially successful, my success attracted other successful, well-educated professionals who wanted to party. I had good friends. I had the wine, women, and song. I had the cars, the wardrobe, the glitzy apartment, and money rolling in, so much so that I would throw it away. Yes, I was the handsome and debonair Latino with money and a penthouse on the beach. I had a sunken aquarium in my living room floor and my own tight gang of friends to share it with. Man, I was something. I could get it done and make it happen. The hype and delusion of the world wrapped me up, and I was lost in the trappings of the fast lane. I consider the years of 1975–1978 as my lost years.

Success and Dangerous Indulgences

I had become accustomed to change. Growing up in Spanish Harlem, I constantly bounced between homes. Although the instability was unsettling, I learned to adapt. I craved action, creativity, culture, and music. I looked for projects and dove into them to consume every minute of my life. I had several other jobs during this time, and sometimes I worked two or three jobs at the same time.

In addition to federal corrections, I worked undercover for the Department of Agriculture and monitored food stamp usage. I caught people and stores using food stamps to buy alcohol and cigarettes instead of food. A private company, Operation SER (Service, Employment, Redevelopment), hired me as a job developer with a specific focus on Hispanics. I placed college graduates into major corporations such as Rohm, General Dynamics, Solar, and Lockheed. Taking advantage of my veteran education benefits, I went to night school for two years. I majored in clinical psychology and obtained an associate degree from San Diego City College.

My love of music naturally led me to producing and promoting concerts at both the San Diego Sports Arena and Jack Murphy Stadium. It was like Woodstock all over again for me. I was in my element. I worked with record executives from London Records, Palador Records, and Mercury Records. I also worked with the musical artists, promoting them and the venues they performed at. Since I had managed the La Bastille nightclub in Houston, the music scene in San Diego was like home. I made sure the artists were taken care of and provided with whatever they needed, no matter how frivolous or ridiculous.

One day, I proposed an idea to the general manager of the San Diego Sports Arena.

I asked, "What if you created a club; a club where, during the Padre games and afterward, people could take a 'time out' to drink and socialize?"

The manager accepted my pitch, and I set up the Time Out Club. I organized intimate social events at the club every other week. I met all kinds of people and made good money.

Pax Productions owner Fred Moore also hired me to promote and put on concerts at the other venue, Jack Murphy Stadium. After the San Diego Padres' game, the arena rolled out a stage and put on concerts for the fans. The Beach Boys performed often, regulars at the stadium. This stadium had a capacity of 55,000. I was involved in the production of the music for the concerts.

The music scene and the association with celebrities drew me into another world and class of people. I was in the world of fame, women, and drugs. In all my time on the streets of New York, at the Woodstock Festival, and in the Marine Corps, my mind and character remained focused and strong. I resisted the lure of drugs. For a while, I was even a drug and alcohol counselor for the NEPSI Narcotics Treatment Program. My best friend Curt was the director of that program and offered me a job there. I also worked in the Methadone Clinic as a counselor. I had knowledge of types of drugs and associated effects. I was educated and trained to identify specific behaviors of drug addicts (such as drowsiness, disorientation, tremors, pinpoint pupils, itching skin, depression, and changes in mood). My job was to help addicts through recovery and treatment programs.

In my social circle, everyone got high and used drugs. I was in the fast lane with my friends, and this world was alluring, seducing, and dangerous. In the mid-1970s, doing drugs was like having hors d'oeuvres and a drink.

I indulged. I did not spiral quickly down a dark tunnel, but my journey was gradual.

I rationalized to myself, "Who am I hurting? It's OK to enjoy yourself and relax."

These were the little lies I told myself. Eventually, I expanded to selling to my professional friends who were doctors, lawyers, and nurses. These people lived in beautiful homes and threw cocktail parties. I was on the go, taking speed for the high to accelerate and perform and then marijuana when I wanted to slow down and chill out. Cocaine (coke) was the rich man's high. Quaaludes enhanced sex. Acid (in a microdot form) caused hallucinations. The acid psychedelic drug LSD, especially, made for a scary trip (LSD's psychological effect is called a "trip"). LSD causes powerful distortions in perceptions, altering any sense of time, and enhancing spiritual experiences. Musicians used LSD to take them to another dimension in their music.

Once I started using drugs, I lived dangerously and took risks that could have killed me or landed me in jail. I went to Tijuana, Mexico, which was a short drive south of San Diego. It was a great place to party, drink, dance, and meet girls in the discos. One of my friends who I met at a disco gave me a bag of cocaine as I left to go back to the US. As I was driving home, I put the small bag of coke on top of my dashboard in between some napkins. Crossing the border, a border patrol agent stopped me for a routine check.

"I need to check your car. Pull over to the side; he'll tell you what to do."

"Open your trunk, I need to look inside," said the other border patrol agent. It was late at night, not a lot of traffic, and he had all the time to do a thorough search.

To distract the agent, I started talking about my time in the Marines. He was interested, and I kept talking, being calm and smooth. All he had to do was look on the dashboard, find the cocaine, and I would have been busted. If drug dogs would have been on duty, the canines would have found the drugs. I was lucky that the agent did not see the small bag of cocaine. I was free to go.

I was a bachelor then and dated a madam in charge of prostitutes in San Diego.

My madam girlfriend asked, "Hey, can you do me a favor? Can you take me and a few of my girls and drop them off at work?"

It wasn't a big deal; just a favor, I thought. As we were driving, I heard police sirens.

"Pull over, *now!*" blared the police car.

Would they think I was the pimp? Would they find the ounce of coke in my sock?

"Everyone, get out of the vehicle," they told us. The police drew their guns and pointed them at us. Four patrol cars surrounded my vehicle. I was shocked but stayed cool as we all slowly stepped out of the car.

"Get your hands up! Get up against the wall! You too!" they shouted.

With guns pointed at us, we did exactly as we were told. We cooperated and kept quiet. I was with the ladies of the night, my face pressed against the wall. As the police frisked me and shook me down, with my hands still up on the wall, I mustered the guts to respectfully ask the cops a question.

"Why did you pull me over?" I whispered respectfully.

"There was a shooting a few blocks away, and you guys fit the description," he stated firmly.

"Officer, would you please look inside my jacket?"

The cop stopped frisking me and looked inside my coat jacket. He fumbled, found my wallet, and flipped it open. He found identification from one of my law enforcement positions. Realizing we were not the shooting suspects, and being distracted talking to me, the police let us go.

"Wow, another close call that could have gone horribly wrong," I thought.

On another occasion, me and my friends were on our way to a party in Imperial Beach, next to Coronado. The host of the party was Cedrick, a marijuana and coke dealer. He was a dark Panamanian who always wore a white Panama hat and sunglasses, even at night. The area of Imperial Beach was a rich area. People with money lived there, and the cops patrolled and kept an eye on the locale.

While driving, I noticed I was being followed. Again, the cops pulled me over. Maybe we looked conspicuous?

My best friends were educated, like me, and had come from the streets, like me. We instinctively knew with a glance what was "going down."

"Everyone, straighten up," I told my friends. Everyone sat up as I instructed, and I slowed the car to a full stop. We were all sober as the police officer approached. The officer looked in the car and spoke to me.

"Where are you going?"

"To a friend's house for a party," I said calmly.

"OK, drive carefully," said the officer, and we were free to go to Cedrick's house.

When we arrived at Cedrick's house, the door was slightly open. My training kicked in, and I sensed that something was not right. It was too quiet, and I did not see Cedrick. Approaching the front door, I slowly pushed it open and called out.

"Cedrick?"

There was no answer. I kept my friends behind me and motioned with my hand to stay behind me and tread lightly. Everyone got the message to be quiet and follow my lead. I entered the home, looking first to my right. In one of the rooms, I found Cedrick and his girlfriend tied up with their mouths bound.

"Man, what happened to you, Cedrick?" I asked.

"Stolen. All my coke and all my money; another gang took it," said Cedrick angrily.

"They had machine guns, Danny, and they surrounded my house, both inside and outside of the house."

We stood, stunned, then untied Cedrick and his girlfriend. The danger of the world of drugs should have sunk in, should have changed my course. We tended to and comforted Cedrick and his girlfriend, both visibly shaken and lucky to be alive. I sidestepped another *very* close call. It could have ended badly. We could have died that night. For sure, Cedrick was lucky to have survived the armed robbery. I never saw him after that night. He moved out— to where I did not know.

Without a doubt in my mind, I know that God protected me that night. What if we had been at Cedrick's house when the other gang arrived? The officer stopping us on the road was God's hand delaying our arrival at Cedrick's and sparing our lives.

I continued networking with people in San Diego and taking on other jobs. For a time, I was the personal bodyguard for Dr. Jonas Salk at his institute in San Diego. I worked for Burns Security and personally escorted Dr. Salk when he was on the grounds of the Salk Institute. At the time, when Dr. Salk talked to me about the polio vaccine and the science behind it, I was not fully aware of the magnitude and reach of his work.

When I was at Salk Institute, I had another close call. Two intruders tried to steal a Salk Institute vehicle. While I was on patrol, I saw them at a distance and started to walk toward them. They panicked, slammed the hood of the car down, and attempted to speed away. As I ran toward the car, they stepped on the accelerator and tried to run me down. I had to dive off to the right to avoid them hitting me. With my radio in my hand, I ran after the car and gave a description to my base headquarters. The police caught them—two foreign students at the University of California, San Diego. After all that, I was promoted to lieutenant and site commander for Salk Institute.

The Power of Praise

In my dealings with people and through the various jobs I held, I noticed how thanking people affected them. I observed that offering a kind word of gratitude changed their disposition and view of themselves. I realized there is real value and power in praise, encouragement, and thanksgiving.

I decided to start a company to acknowledge people, to thank them for their achievements. I founded the International Latin Academy Awards, Inc. to promote God, humanity, and the arts. I wanted to help other people who had good ideas and talent but who never really had an opportunity to express their talent. I wanted to thank and acknowledge people for their good work and contributions. Doors opened. I was in the right place at the right time—God's time and place.

Diplomatic Mentors, Mr. and Mrs. Alexander

Sometimes for dinner, my friends and I would cross the border into Tijuana, Mexico. One night, three of us went to a posh, elegant Mexican restaurant. We were in white shirts, suits, and ties. A pair of well-dressed gentlemen who worked for the Mexican government started a conversation and asked us if we wanted to go to a party up the street. We were up for it and said yes.

The home where the party was held was a secure estate shaped like a half-moon. The structure was built up from the rocky beach below and sat high on a cliff overlooking the ocean. The balcony view of the ocean was panoramic. From the balcony, one could watch dolphins dancing in the water. The inside was like a palace, furnished with plush furniture spaciously laid out on marble floors. Wow, I thought, this guy has got to have a lot of money.

A petite and stunning older Black woman answered the door. Her name was Mrs. Alexander.

"Who are you?" she asked.

"I am Danny Garcia, and I am president of the International Latin Academy Awards. These are two of my friends and associates."

Mrs. A., as I called her, took us around and introduced us to her guests. I did not know where I was or who these people were, but I talked with the partygoers. They were mostly white, sophisticated, educated, well-groomed, and polished like our host. These guests were from San Antonio Del Mar, an elite place in Baja, California, where Americans with means lived. My African American friend Paul Sims, my French friend Bashar, and I stood out from the crowd. Paul was an important man in San Diego County, and Bashar had a business enterprise.

We were a dynamic and mixed trio. Immediately, people were drawn to us. I did my thing, mingling, socializing, and entertaining them. We were the last to leave the party, and that's when Mrs. A. approached me.

"Who, really, are you? Mr. Alexander wants to know. We want to know how you did it. You successfully crashed our party. In fact, you took over. How did you do it? Mr. A. said he would like you to come back and talk with him."

When we left, Paul told me, "If I were you, I would come back. These people really like you." I did return to the estate, and the Alexanders wanted to know more about me. I had charm and charisma. I knew how to hold a conversation and how to carry myself. Bud Roberts taught me and groomed me well.

I discovered that Mr. Sanford Alexander was a diplomat, the Consul General of Grenada to Mexico. His residence was in

Tijuana. Grenada is a Caribbean nation and known as the "Spice Isle." He was an important man, and wherever he went in Baja, people excitedly welcomed him. Mr. A. was wealthy, successful, and generous. His wife, Mrs. A., a political leader and powerful woman, was completely devoted to him. Neither of them had children, although they wanted them.

Like Bud Roberts, Mr. A. took a liking to me and adopted me as a son. He marveled at my ideas and vision for the International Latin Academy Awards and was one of the few people who believed in me. He embraced me and coached me like a son. He exposed me to the people, places, and politics of his diplomatic world. Mr. A. taught me how to carry myself as a diplomat. He loved me, and Mrs. A. loved me too. They both supported my dreams and aspirations. They hoped I would fill a gap, a void in their life. In me, he saw a tremendous amount of faith. He was excited about my boldness, the same boldness I showed when I crashed their party.

"This is Danny, my son." This is how Mr. A. introduced me to his guests. I would call him Dad too.

The Alexanders entertained frequently and were hospitable to everyone. I soon became the trusted driver who picked up visiting diplomats in San Diego and brought them to official meetings at the Consulate of Grenada in Tijuana. I drove two classic black Lincoln Continental limousines. The Alexanders went first class in everything and were known as the crème de la crème. For example, when the Mexican restaurant down the street was to host a dignitary, such as the governor, the restaurant would ask to borrow the Alexanders' silverware.

Like Bud, Mr. A. had a legacy to pass on. He envisioned me visiting Grenada one day with him to see his birthplace, where a street is named after him. He had wealth, prestige, and wisdom to give to a son. For example, Mr. A. told me he was the first man to establish a showroom for cars in Los Angeles. He also owned his own newspaper business. He offered to bestow his legacy upon me and to introduce me to other important people.

On one occasion, Mr. A. coordinated a trip for me to go to New York and meet the first prime minister of Grenada, Sir Eric Matthew Gairy. Sir Gairy served as the first prime minister of Grenada after it gained independence from Britain in 1974. I went to the United Nations and heard Sir Gairy speak in 1979. He was one of the most eloquent speakers I had ever heard. Afterward, Sir Gairy invited me to a private party for his guests, and I met people from different countries. I presented Sir Gairy with an award, then flew back and thanked the Alexanders for the gracious opportunity at the UN.

Mr. and Mrs. A. were special to me, and I to them. I felt their love in every conversation and in every moment I spent with them. I didn't ask for anything, but they always treated me well and took care of me. We continued the relationship, and I traveled on weekends back and forth from San Diego to Tijuana for a few years. They knew I had my own life in San Diego and responsibilities with the International Latin Academy Awards, and they respected that obligation. My visits became more infrequent.

One day, I went back to see the Alexanders. Mrs. A. was distraught with grief, searching for words. She mournfully struggled to tell me that the love of her life, Mr. A., had died.

"Why didn't you tell me?" I felt like I had no air. I sat down and regrouped.

All the plans and visions we had together suddenly evaporated, just like that. Mrs. A. was empty and totally lost without Mr. A.

"I'll be here for you, whatever you need Mrs. A. Please call me," I said.

I made sure she had my contact information and left, deeply troubled that my father figure had died. Several months later, Mrs. A. also passed.

Thank You, Jackie O.

Back in San Diego, I received a call one day from NBC in New York City. The man's name was Felipe Luciano, and he was producing the Latin Roots Exhibit. Felipe invited me to attend a reception and to preview the exhibit displaying the Spanish music history in New York from 1930–1978. It was held at the Library of Performing Arts at the Lincoln Center. My father, Jose "Bilingue" Garcia, among many others, such as Tito Puente and Billy Taylor, was to be honored for their contributions to American music in New York from the 1930s through the late 1970s. My father was too ill to attend, so I was invited to represent Jose "Bilingue" Garcia. It was September 1978.

Jackie Kennedy Onassis was scheduled to arrive to view the exhibit, and I had a small award to thank her. As soon as word spread of the icon's arrival, everyone rushed to the entrance of the Lincoln Center to get a glimpse of Jackie O. But I stayed back, not joining the clamorous crowd. Instead, I positioned myself at the top of the steps near the exit of the exhibit. A journalist, Ross Najarean, noticed the award in my hand and inquired, "What's that?"

"It's an award for Jackie, for acknowledging my father and all the pioneers of the Latin Roots Exhibit," I explained.

Ross screamed out to the crowd, "Jackie's gonna receive an award!"

That was it. Frenzied photographers ran past the former First Lady toward me and knelt at my feet as Jackie O. approached me at the top of the stairs where I was standing and patiently waiting.

I addressed the former First Lady. "Jackie, I would like to present this gift to you on behalf of my father and the International Latin Academy Awards."

Jackie Onassis was the first person to receive an award of thanks from my organization. As I raised the small glass award to hand it to her, she touched it delicately with her right hand and fixed her delighted gaze upon my gift. There I was, face-to-face with one of the most famous ladies of our time, to give her a gift and to acknowledge her.

With the elegance and grace for which she is historically famous, Jackie said kindly, "Thank you." The same journalist who alerted the crowd, Ross Najarian of the Inquirer, captured that moment of Jackie O.'s acceptance and of my thanks and gratitude in an article titled "Jackie Says 'Saludos, Amigos,' at Latin Exhibit."

Presenting Award to Jackie Kennedy Onassis (1978)

None of this was scripted or planned. God orchestrated this meeting with Mrs. Onassis, and that picture went all over the world. Afterward, I continued to travel and thank famous people with gifts of gratitude. My vision was to reach everyone, male or female, rich or poor, young or old, famous or unknown, and lift them with two simple words: "*thank you.*"

President Carter

During 1978, I continued to recognize and thank dignitaries who had an impact on the Latin community through my company, the International Latin Academy Awards. President Jimmy Carter, for example, negotiated a year earlier (September 1977) the Panama Canal treaty which gave Panama full control of the Panama Canal after the year 1999. An eighty-four-year-old Latino poet, Antonio Perez, impressed upon me the significance of the Panama Canal Treaty to Latin countries. We then drove 3,000 miles to Washington, D.C. with no appointment to say thank you to the president.

Some in the State Department and the Washington Post staff thought we were crazy. They laughed at us. I called the White House and left messages, but it seemed we had reached a dead end. We were exhausted, dejected, and depressed. I cried out to God.

"God, why did you bring me all this way and I can't get into the White House?"

Then the phone rang. It was the White House—the president's secretary, Catalina Espinosa. I explained to her that we had a poem and an award for the president and had traveled a very long way with just enough money to drive back to California. I did not want to bother anyone but was at the end of my rope, ready to go home.

"Mr. Garcia, don't do that. Let me see what I can do. Can you wait one more day?"

We stayed one more day, then Catalina called me.

"Can you come to the White House tomorrow morning?" she asked.

"Of course, yes, thank you," I said.

At that time, President Carter was concluding the Camp David Accords, a historic Middle East peace agreement between Egypt's Anwar Sadat and Israel's Menachem Begin. He was not at the White House, so I did not meet with the president. Rather, I made the presentation, a Human Rights Award, and Ms. Espinosa accepted the gifts on the president's behalf. It was another door of favor that opened, and we accomplished the mission. To get home after the presentation, Antonio used his social security check. The president signed a nice letter on the White House stationery thanking me for the Human Rights Award in recognition of the president's efforts in negotiating the new Panama Canal treaties.

THE WHITE HOUSE

WASHINGTON

October 12, 1978

To Daniel Garcia

Thank you very much for the Human
Rights Award, which you and your
associates in the International
Latin Academy bestowed on me in
recognition of my efforts in
negotiating the new Panama Canal
Treaties.

I appreciate your thoughtfulness.

Sincerely,

Jimmy Carter

Mr. Daniel Garcia
President
International Latin Awards, Inc.
Suite 206
4155 West Point Loma Boulevard
San Diego, California 92110

Letter from President Jimmy Carter

Goodbye, Papi

Shortly after the presentation to President Carter, I received devastating news that my father had died from cancer. He passed on September 26, 1978. I was not able to see him before he died. I never had the chance to say, "Thank you, Papi. I love you."

My heart was broken. I questioned my own mortality and regretted the time lost with my father. I did not know him, really, and that saddened me. I also thought of the parallel with my own estranged children and how I missed them. At his graveside, as my Papi was being lowered into his grave, I placed a medal on the casket.

"Papi, I present this award to you on behalf of the International Latin Academy Awards."

I said goodbye in my heart—I had no more words. Only after his death did I understand the breadth of his contributions to Latin music in New York City. As an accomplished percussionist, he was part of the pioneering movement of musicians who introduced the Cuban musical combination of congas, bongos, and timbales unique to Latin jazz. In addition to playing with Machito and the Afro-Cubans and Xavier Cugat, my father performed with other well-known artists. This list includes Desi Arnez, Alberto Socarrás (flautist), Noro Morales (pianist), Chano Pozo (congas), Miguelito Valdés, Panchito Riset, and Mongo Santamaría.

I reflected on the fact that, as a dark-skinned man, my father had to enter the venues through the back door. Being Afro-Cuban and bilingual, my father straddled several ethnic worlds: Cuban, African American, and Hispanic. He taught me the concept of respectability—having it, keeping it, and giving it. He taught me how to get along with people of many different colors. In many ways, I am my father's son.

As I dealt with the finality of my father's life, as well as the passing of both Mr. and Mrs. Alexander, I heard God. God called out to me in such sorrowful moments, whispering to my spirit, "Come to me, my son."

Little Revelations of God

When I returned to San Diego, I caught a ride from a nice lady named Linda who introduced me to a spiritual book titled *Letters of the Scattered Brotherhood.* This book was an unexpected vehicle of His calling; unexpected because I did not like to read. It was also extraordinary for two reasons: one, that I considered reading it at all; and two, that once I started reading the book, I read it completely, cover to cover. I found deep, profound truths within its pages. I kept the book in my very limited library, and I read it over and over again.

What was unique about the book was that the editor intentionally kept anonymous the names of the authors and the dates of the writings. No matter what page I opened to, the words seemed to relate specifically to me, with spiritual revelations just for me. Toward the end of the book, one of the letters described concentric circles of existence and personal cognizance of events, chaos, and reaction to stimuli. The author advised to guard one's center, one's thoughts, and refers to the center of peace that encircles the universe.

I believed the author referred to the Kingdom of God. The concepts were ethereal and insightful. I had never read or been taught such themes. The visual of being in the center of the universe resonated with me. The truths in the book transformed my thinking and what I cared about. The Lord used this book to bring His presence to my consciousness. My life also dramatically changed after I read *Letters of the Scattered Brotherhood.* God gave me a clear revelation about being in His center and using artwork to reveal love and truth.

At this time in my life, I had this awareness of God because of my Catholic upbringing. I did not, however, have a real relationship with Him. The life and close calls described in this chapter opened my ears to hear God speaking to me. God never abandoned me. Rather, I rejected and ignored Him. I convinced myself that I knew better and that my choices were better than His.

I was lost during these years, 1975–1978. The trappings of the world consumed me. I thought I had it all, but I had nothing.

In 1979, I became more involved with church. More revelations materialized as I sought to promote children, and that work led me to meet His Holiness Pope John Paul II.

CHAPTER 6:

The Pope and *The Child*

This chapter is devoted to the times that I interacted with His Holiness Pope John Paul II.

In late 1978, although I experienced more and more spiritual revelations, I still ran hard in the fast lane. I was either throwing parties at my home or partying at the Time Out Club. A local artist arrived unexpectedly at one of my private events and wanted to talk with me. He did not have money to pay to get into the party, but he had an ounce of marijuana. He was a fellow Latino, so I let him in, and we talked. He was a painter who created huge murals on buildings in San Diego and in the Southern California area.

After a few minutes, the artist said, "I want to invite you to my house to see my paintings."

I agreed to visit him and view his work. He showed me a variety of his works of art that were on display in his house, but I was more interested in the large murals he painted on the buildings in San Diego.

I asked the artist, "I am looking for something that we could share with the whole world and present to the United Nations in New York. Can you do it?"

The artist was puzzled and asked, "Danny, how are you going to get into the UN?" Although he grappled with that question, he said OK. He agreed to create a painting.

From 1979–1996, I embarked on an extensive project to promote the artist. I committed time and resources, a valuable investment, which allowed me to visit places such as Mexico, the Vatican, Israel, Korea, and Bosnia.

Puebla, Mexico

The first opportunity was in January 1979. My local church sponsored a trip to Mexico for me to present to Pope John Paul II a painting: *La Virgen de Guadalupe* (originally a mural in Chicano Park under the Coronado Bridge in San Diego). Pope John Paul II was touring Latin America and was to address the Third General Conference of the Latin American Episcopate on January 28, 1979, in Puebla, a city sixty-six miles southeast of Mexico City.

Every avenue I tried to get to the pope was blocked. In Puebla, I asked a bishop if I could present the painting, and he told me the pope was having an audience for a one-million-dollar donor. I did not have that kind of money.

I sat in my hotel room, frustrated, near tears, and watching the crowds on television. Fortunately, a Mexican reporter reached out to me on the phone out of the blue.

"I heard you have a gift for the pope," he said. I was shocked and marveled at how the reporter knew of my quest and how to reach me. I was a nobody. He told me where the pope was going to be and suggested I just go there. I caught a cab to the square, estimated to be jammed with more than one million people waiting to welcome the pope, who was popular with Mexico's huge number of Roman Catholics.

"How are we going to get through all these people?" I asked.

"Come on, we'll walk you through," said the cab driver and his wife.

We walked arm-in-arm, me in the middle holding the painting and the cab driver and his wife on either side of me, carrying a portfolio of letters. As the crowd looked at the painting and at the three of us, they stepped aside and made way for us. They parted like the Red Sea—a miracle, I thought. We continued to march forward until the police stopped us.

"Who are you and why are you here?" asked the Mexican police.

Before I could speak, the cab driver unfastened my portfolio. It fell open to the letter I had received from President Jimmy Carter. They were surprised and immediately impressed. They read "The White House" and saw the signature of the president of the United States.

"An emissary from the president of the United States! Clear the way," instructed the police. They then escorted me to the door of the meeting place of the pope and the bishops' conference.

While I did not have an audience with the pope that day, I successfully delivered the painting to someone who did present it on my behalf.

UNESCO declared 1979 as the International Year of the Child (IYC), and UNICEF led the IYC activities, twenty years after the Declaration of the Rights of the Child. This same year, the same artist finished a four-by-four-foot painting titled *The Child* in commemoration of children around the world. Numerous newspaper articles chronicled the journey of *The Child*, and many news articles focused on the vision of presenting the painting to the pope.

I stared at *The Child* in amazement. I studied the child sitting in the center of the universe, perched safely in the palm of a majestic hand with circles surrounding the child and expanding outward. I had a revelation. The *Letters of the Scattered Brotherhood* described circles of existence and the center of calm and stillness as the kingdom of heaven. This was no coincidence—God was talking to me. And I had a question for Him.

"What do you want me to do with this painting?" I asked God.

As I talked to God, I noticed that supernatural things were happening all around me. God caught my attention. He gave me a grand vision of spreading a message of peace to the children of the world.

With new vigor, I established a nonprofit organization: Children of Our World. I devoted all my energy and creativity to a full-blown production and promotion of *The Child*. My idea was to present the painting to the United Nations in conjunction with the International Year of the Child.

"It's a bold idea, but how are we going to get in?" the artist continued to ask me.

"God will get me in. I just have to go, and He will open the doors."

By faith, I went to New York City with *The Child*. Arriving in New York City in September 1979 with no plan and no place to stay, I sought help. Somehow, I met the monsignor of St. Stanislaus, a Polish Catholic church in lower Manhattan. I shared my idea of presenting *The Child* at the United Nations. The church allowed me to display the painting for 1,000 school children. The children wrote about their thoughts of the painting.

I asked children, "In this painting, who do you think the child is?"

Many of the children said, "It is baby Jesus."

In the original painting, the child had a halo about its head. I believed *The Child* visually conveyed the message that children are the future, and the future is in God's hands.

The monsignor said, "Pope John Paul II will be coming to New York to speak at the UN on Oct 2nd [1979]. Can you stay with me at the church for a couple of days? The kids and I can pray for you that God will open the doors."

"Yes, monsignor, what do you want me to do?"

"Wait," he said assuredly.

The monsignor provided a room for me at the church while he made an appointment to see the Apostolic Mission to the UN. Together, we took the painting and told the story of *The Child* to the archbishop. The archbishop was a diplomatic representative of the Holy See (the equivalent of an embassy).

"Leave the painting with me," the archbishop said to me. "The pope has a meeting here before he speaks at the UN. I'll show him the painting."

Meanwhile, the UN raised the security level because Fidel Castro of Cuba was also scheduled to visit the UN at the same time. The monsignor came back to the parish and advised me that the painting was at the Holy See Mission and that the archbishop intended to show it to the pope. This was God's plan, and I had the faith to follow His lead.

Several days later, Pope John Paul II, sitting in the archbishop's parlor, turned around and saw the painting. He immediately commented favorably and asked questions about *The Child* and about me. I was told the pope remembered me from Puebla, Mexico, where I delivered the painting *La Virgen de Guadalupe* to His Holiness. Shortly thereafter, I was told, the pope asked that the Holy See write a letter introducing the painting and me to UNICEF at the United Nations. I was shocked that the pope remembered me and cleared the way for me to make my presentation to the United Nations.

How? What? Where? When? Who? I was both incredulous and electrified when I was summoned to the UN, bearing a letter from the Holy See introducing me to present *The Child* to the United Nations. God was faithful, and he honored my faith and the prayers of the children. I presented the painting as a symbol of children and peace, and *The Child* was on exhibition for a year at the office of the International Year of the Child secretariat at the UN.

Mr. John Grun, former director of the International Year of the Child secretariat, pulled me aside at the United Nations.

He spoke to me with amazement and asked, "Do you know this is a miracle? How did you do it? How is it that the pope would see and ask about *The Child*, remember you, and ask that a letter of introduction be made on your behalf?"

"There have been a lot of kids who prayed that the UN would receive this painting," I replied to John Grun. "God used Pope John Paul II to help me get in and present it to you and to the children of the world."

People wanted to believe that I somehow orchestrated the events, and I reminded them in the words of Jesus, "Nothing is impossible with God."

Rome, The Vatican

I also worked with the Knights of Columbus at the parish I attended, where the painting was on display. With the help of Grand Knight John Moore, I was determined to have the original of *The Child* presented to the pope in Rome. The Knights of Columbus had an audience scheduled with the pope, and after seven years of planning, *The Child* was presented in 1985 at the Vatican, where the original four-by-four painting resides today.

God orchestrated another opportunity for me to meet Pope John Paul II again in Rome in 1988. I had a small, framed replica of *The Child* for His Holiness. I stood a few feet from him. As I held the painting in my left hand, the pope looked down upon it and smiled. He raised his right hand to bless the gift and then placed his left hand upon my right wrist. The Pontiff held on to me for a few moments while he studied the painting. I was in the presence of greatness and spiritual humility, a time I will never forget.

Later, the artist painted *The Child* as a fourteen-by-forty-eight-foot mural on vinyl material at Gannet Outdoor Advertising Company in San Diego. To maximize exposure and to spread the message of peace, I displayed *The Child* mural at the border entering Tijuana, Mexico, (Dec 1990) and at the Holland Tunnel in New York City.

The last encounter with Pope John Paul II was in December 1998—Christmas time. I was honored to receive a letter from the Vatican secretariat of state thanking me for other gifts I presented to Pope John Paul II in Rome. Although I did not see him in person, the Vatican secretary of state, Monsignor Pedro Lopez Quintana, wrote me a beautiful letter of gratitude on behalf of the Pontiff.

For some reason, I felt a connection with Pope John Paul II. As I stepped out in faith to support children, I believed the Spirit of God gave me supernatural favor with the Pontiff. He helped me, and for that, I am grateful and blessed to have met him personally.

To travel around the world promoting *The Child*, a generous sponsor supported me. Lorella Losa introduced me to a local outstanding businessman: Jerome V. Stapp II of New Century Securities, Inc. He read about me in the papers and wanted to meet me. He was an avid supporter of the Boys & Girls Club of Oceanside, California. Once I told Jerry what I wanted to do, he supported me. A World War II veteran who fought at the Battle of the Bulge and Normandy, Jerry was one of the leading fundraisers and supporters of the Boys & Girls Club. He read about me in the papers, believed in me, and decided to support me. Jerry was incredibly generous and provided $200,000 (this is not a misprint, $200,000) to help me travel abroad.

I summarized and extracted in this chapter the amazing encounters I had with Pope John Paul II from 1979–1990. What an incredible servant of God. Chronologically in this story, though, I must step back to 1979. A radically different course and purpose unfolded that year, the very purpose for which God created me. That event was my transformation.

CHAPTER 7:

"You Must Choose Now"

Returning to the year 1979, I recollected that I had an awareness of God because of my Catholic upbringing. I did not, however, have a real relationship with him. The life and close calls described previously opened my ears to hear God speaking to me. God never abandoned me. Rather, I rejected and ignored Him. I convinced myself that I knew better and that my choices were better than His.

After presenting *The Child* to the UN in the fall of 1979, I went home to San Diego and got back into my groove, my lifestyle. In my apartment in El Cajon, I continued to get high. To the public, I was a man working with church and UN officials and speaking for children's rights. In private, though, I was different. I knew the difference between right and wrong, but I was disobedient and chose my way. I was separated but living as a bachelor. I smoked grass, dealt drugs, partied, and lived dangerously. To relax after a full day, I filled my evenings listening to music. I drank alcohol, smoked a joint, or took other drugs such as cocaine.

I was under grace, but not aware of that awesome gift.

One night in my living room, under the influence of several drugs and alcohol, I experienced something bizarre and frightening. Something happened to me, and I knew that something was terribly wrong. In a moment, I felt my spirit leaving my body; a wrenching separation and tearing from deep within. Life literally came out of my body. My feet lifted from the floor. I levitated upwards and felt myself being pulled out of this world. It was an out-of-body experience. I did not feel physical pain, but I knew I was dying. All my life, I had been in control and never let fear consume me. Now, I was terrified.

I panicked.

My thoughts raced. I knew that if I died, I would go to hell because of all the bad things I had done in my life. I learned in Catholic school that if I died in the state of mortal sin, I was destined for hell, a place of eternal fire and torment. Eternity flashed before me, and I heard an audible voice through time, space, and spirit say:

"Which way do you choose? Life or death? *You must choose now.*"

The voice enveloped my thoughts. In a flash, the Lord gave me a choice of life or death, and it was a choice of both physical and spiritual proportions. Although I had not been in church for over twenty-five years, I knew I was lost, had no hope, and was going to hell. I was completely petrified, and for the first time in my entire life, I was truly afraid and frightened beyond my understanding.

With a desperate cry, I screamed, "*Jesus, save me!*"

As soon as I said the name "Jesus," my spirit immediately jumped back into my body. I experienced the terrible fear of God. To this point in my life, I paid no attention to the teachings that the Catholic church instilled in me. I had turned away from Him and disobeyed His laws.

By calling on the name of Jesus Christ, I chose life. I was saved spiritually; the moment of my salvation from death and beginning the transformation to a new life. *This was a miracle.* I was thirty-three years old—the same age as Jesus when he started his public ministry.

My girlfriend at the time was in another room. She found me and frantically called the paramedics. The ambulance rushed me to the hospital where I was shot up with all kinds of sedatives. The hospital staff concluded that I had a severe anxiety attack. Was it just a bad acid trip? Did the dealer sell me drugs laced with something bad? The hospital knew nothing else, including what drugs I had taken that night. To alleviate my fear and anxiety, the doctor prescribed Sinequan, an antidepressant (one pill every four hours was the usual dosage; the doctor prescribed several more to sedate me). Antidepressants increased the risk of suicidal thoughts or actions.

I Was a Vegetable

I was under medical supervision and taking prescription drugs for a year. I was a vegetable, not able to care for myself or to go to the bathroom by myself. I was fearful and suffered from agoraphobia, trembling and sweating every day. My symptoms intensified when I left my apartment. I dreaded social interaction and being outside my home alone. Even though my girlfriend took care of me, I wanted to die.

During this year, I was afraid of doing anything wrong (drugs, sleeping around), and afraid of God's punishment and banishment to hell. Everything stopped. My friends would drop by, concerned, not knowing what happened to me and why I had so drastically changed. I remember someone giving me a joint. I smoked it and got dizzy and nauseous.

"I told you. Stop it," the spiritual voice warned me.

This was God's voice speaking to me.

There was nowhere to run or hide. I tried, but could not get away from the hounds of heaven. God knew all my thoughts. I could not trick Him or talk my way out of His presence. I gave in and quit trying to fool Him. My guilt was overwhelming. After my life-and-death experience, I evaluated my life and asked myself some profound questions:

"How did I get *here*?"

"What happened to me?"

"How did my life get to this point?"

"Where can I go for help?"

The doctors and the antidepressants were not working. Reality? Insanity? I could not distinguish between what was real and what were hallucinations. I couldn't live in the madness and wanted to end it all, to commit suicide. I did not believe I could change my life for the better. I realized I needed help that medical doctors could not provide.

I went to the one place that would help me: a house of God. The church was a Catholic church, Our Lady of Grace. There I found charismatics, those who believed in the power and gifts of the Holy Spirit. I walked in, told them I was sick and asked for prayer. This was the first time I met charismatic Christians who prayed over me.

The charismatics gathered around me, laid hands on me, and prayed in tongues (a heavenly spiritual language). God answered their prayers, and I experienced another spiritual event: the cloudy darkness which enclosed around and smothered me, the spirit of death and thoughts of suicide, left me. Everything evil and dark vanished from my inner being and I was filled with light. The spirit of life surrounded me with peace and serenity. I felt complete again, whole and healed.

My thirst and search for Jesus grew rapidly and led me to a second encounter with the charismatics during a church service. They preached about being "born again," and I had never heard this message.

What a revelation! I was all-in and convicted on the spot. In the middle of a service of about one hundred people, I stood up and shouted for all to hear.

"I want to confess! I'm sorry for what I've done; I want to be born again. I want to receive Jesus, and I want to be free!"

The parishioners were shocked; no one ever stood up and interrupted a Catholic service. Graciously, the charismatic believers prayed for me, and this time I participated in a specific prayer called the "Sinner's Prayer." I received Jesus as my Lord and Savior.

God took Danny Garcia, the confident and worldly concert producer, and transformed him into Danny Garcia, a follower of Jesus Christ. It was both dramatic and traumatic. For the first time in my life, I felt true *fear*. I had never experienced this in the streets, in the Vietnam theater, or during many of my dangerously narrow escapes. I experienced the fear of God.

After I accepted Jesus, I was a new person. But my personal life was in shambles. With my new perspective, I was convicted of my sinful life. I repented (turned in the other direction) from my evil ways. I was not on easy street and, in fact, my life became worse. I went through episodes of disbelief and rejection from others who did not understand my conversion. I dealt with the real and ongoing consequences of the sins I had committed. The consequences did not magically evaporate. I had to learn how to forgive myself and address the aftermath of my decisions.

For example, I was still living with my girlfriend. My encounters with the pope touched me spiritually and shone a light on my sin. I was convicted that living together without being married did not please God. I could not even touch her in that state of sin. The weight of guilt was heavy on my heart. I was determined to get my life straight.

"I have to go," I told my girlfriend. I packed two suitcases and got in the car. "Just take me to Our Lady of Grace church and leave me there on the doorstep."

Monsignor Maloney was taking confessions when I arrived. It was an open confessional with a screen that separated me from the Monsignor. I revealed to the Monsignor that I left my girlfriend and wanted to stop doing drugs. I had an ounce of marijuana on me.

"Monsignor Maloney," I confided. "This is marijuana. I don't want it. Take it from me."

"Is this real?" The Monsignor seemed puzzled and curious, as if he was unfamiliar with drugs, with people like me, and the type of life I lived. "How much is this worth?"

"Yes, it is real, and that bag is worth about two hundred dollars," I informed him. "Anyway, I came to tell you, Monsignor, that I can't live in sin, so I left my girlfriend."

"Danny, it is ok. You are under God's grace. Go, stay with her, and you can be married later. I'll let you know when I will marry you."

I responded, "I can't live that way, and I can't go back. That's why I came here to the church. I can sleep here until something comes up. I know God will provide."

As we talked, a man who was in the church service when I accepted Jesus saw me. Dick Shenk witnessed my bold declaration of faith and remembered me. That boldness spoke to him about his own level of faith. Dick heard some of my conversation with the Monsignor and was intrigued.

Hearing my plight, Dick said, "Danny, come with me."

Dick was a bachelor and had room in his home and an extra car. He took me to a supermarket, asked me what I liked to eat, and bought groceries. I was a stranger, and Dick took me in. He showed me my room and provided food and shelter. I needed a place to stay, and God provided through Dick.

Dick reassured me, "Don't worthy about anything, Danny."

Spiritual Attack, Bound and Gagged

I was committed to Jesus. The devil was angry and came after me. That first night at Dick's house, while I was watching TV, something that I could not see attacked me. It grabbed me and held me down tightly so that I could not move my arms. I remembered a few words of the charismatics' prayer.

"I rebuke you in the name of Jesus!"

I said these words with authority. The force released me, and I ran into Dick's room. I woke him up and told him about the dark encounter. We knelt at his bedside and prayed.

The next night, it happened again. The devil attacked me, but this time the force not only bound me but gagged my mouth. I felt a powerful, large hand covering my mouth so that I couldn't speak.

With my mind and my thoughts, I proclaimed, "I rebuke you in the name of Jesus!"

The unseen assailant left me, and I was freed. That's when I realized there are two worlds: the physical one we see with our eyes, and another spiritual world we cannot see.

In 1982, I officially divorced my first wife. Then, at the end of that year, Monsignor Maloney married me and my girlfriend. She had been with me through my life-and-death experience and cared for me when I was an invalid. I grew to love her because of her kindness.

In the meantime, professionally, I left the music, entertainment, and drug scenes. As mentioned in a previous chapter, I devoted my time and efforts toward promoting *The Child* and messages of peace and became more involved with the church. My family and I lived in a Christian community, like a kibbutz, at 1640 S Pacific Street in Oceanside, where my dear friend, Lorella Losa, took care of us. At that property, Lorella nurtured the spiritual growth and gifts of a unique group of Christians. Faith abounded and many miracles occurred. While living at the 1640 property, I also met a former Marine, Chris Taliaferro, and his wife, Lisa. Chris was like a brother to me and understood the conflict brewing as I drew closer to God and away from past worldly desires. Chris and Lisa honored me when they asked me to be the godfather to their youngest son.

The Queen of England

Meanwhile, at my church, the pastor made an unusual request. "Danny, we have a woman in the church who wants to meet the Queen of England when she visits San Diego. I want you to help her."

I asked the pastor, "How am I going to do that? I don't know the Queen. I don't even have a job."

"You, Danny, have a lot of faith," he answered. "You live a life of miracles." The pastor then introduced me to this special woman.

Vickie Thrift, a mother of four, was a fan of Queen Elizabeth and had been writing to the monarch since 1952. Buckingham Palace, the Queen's lady-in-waiting, always responded to her letters. Vickie's lifelong dream was to meet the Queen. So, I picked up the phone and put my PR skills to work. I contacted the media, City Hall, the British Consul General's office in Los Angeles, and other politicians.

"The Queen is a guest of President Reagan, and a special meeting would be all but impossible to arrange," said the British Consul General's office. "You would need special permission from the White House." We needed help from the office of the president.

"There are two levels of people, a queen and a housewife. It would take a miracle for those two to meet on the same ground," I told a newspaper reporter.

And then the miracle happened.

Senator Peter Wilson stepped in and wrote a letter to the President's staff asking for that special meeting for Vickie. Vickie received one of two hundred invitations to meet Queen Elizabeth in Balboa Park on February 26, 1983. Because I had made Vickie somewhat of a celebrity in her hometown of Santee, I was also invited. Before the meeting, we received special instructions on how to behave, how to address her, and how to conduct ourselves respectfully. We were ecstatic. Queen Elizabeth II, "the first reigning British monarch to visit San Diego," and Prince Philip arrived in her Yacht Britannia to the cheers of thousands on Broadway Pier.

At Balboa Park, Vickie and I prepared for our encounter with the Queen. When our opportunity came, I introduced Vickie to Queen Elizabeth.

"Your Majesty, I would like to present Mrs. Vickie Thrift, the woman who has been writing to you since 1952," I announced.

Then, I stepped back and let Vickie take center stage, and she expressed her love for the Queen. It was a magnificent moment. When I met Queen Elizabeth, her elegance, dignity, grace, and charm overwhelmed me. I was deeply humbled and honored.

Yes, I met the Queen of England and shook her hand.

San Diego took notice and acknowledged my special missions for God, humanity, and the arts. In fact, Mayor Maureen O'Connor issued a proclamation declaring the month of June 1987 as "Dan Garcia Month" to recognize my contributions.

The City of San Diego

Proclamation

Presented By
The Office Of
The Mayor

WHEREAS, Dan Garcia, a San Diegan, embarked on a special mission in 1979; and

WHEREAS, Dan Garcia went on a mission to Rome, Italy to present a painting of the Holy Child by a local San Diego artist to the Pope; and

WHEREAS, Dan Garcia's seven-year journey which culminated in the fall of 1985, included the presentation of the painting to numerous churches and the United Nations Building in New York City; and

WHEREAS, Dan Garcia's life has been characterized by a fervent promotion of God, humanity, and the arts;

NOW, THEREFORE, I, MAUREEN O'CONNOR, the Thirty-first Mayor of the City of San Diego, do hereby proclaim June, 1987 to be "DAN GARCIA MONTH" in San Diego, and commend him for his efforts to help promote peace in the world.

IN WITNESS WHEREOF, I HAVE HEREUNTO SET MY HAND, THIS DAY, AND HAVE CAUSED THE SEAL TO BE AFFIXED HERETO:

MAUREEN O'CONNOR
MAYOR

June 5, 1987
DATE

Dan Garcia Month Declaration (June 1987)

I traveled extensively and presented, either in person or through intermediaries, approximately four hundred symbols of peace to dignitaries and world leaders on behalf of the Children for World Peace Foundation, financed by Jerry Stabb II. He sponsored a tour of peace where I took *The Child* on a world tour to places such as the Vatican in Italy, the Olympics in Korea, and the Royal Family in London, England.

This was the time when I began to focus on promoting peace and children's rights internationally. The first leg was to the religious cities of Rome and Tel Aviv.

As I mentioned before, I had met Pope John Paul II again in Rome, then proceeded to Israel.

Israel, Prime Minister Shamir and Ancient Masada

A tour guide, Jewel Demar Chese, arranged my first trip to Israel. Jewel created a private excursion where I was one of a handful of people chosen as an emissary for more than a standard site-seeing tour. Jewel designed the tour for us to meet with government officials, spread the message of peace, and promote the rights of children around the world. Press had already covered my impending visit. Would I experience a miracle and secure an audience with the prime minister?

Jewel was well-known and had many connections in Israel. She was a cultured woman of influence. When I told her that I wanted to present a reproduction of *The Child* to the prime minister, Jewel said she could help me get an audience with him, Yitzhak Shamir, a legendary and historical figure.

Jewel was protective and careful. She did a thorough background check on me and ensured I was the real deal. The screening process Jewel conducted had to pass the standards of Israeli security, one of the most stringent and effective processes in the world.

Since I asked for a meeting with the leader of Israel, there were many sensitivities to consider. There could be no mistakes, no hidden agendas, no threat to the head of state. In faith, we set off to Israel believing God would open the door to the prime minister.

Jewel's navigation through Israeli security, cabinet approvals, and administrators was masterful. When we arrived in Israel, we lodged in one of the most luxurious and plush hotels, the King David. I was treated like royalty. When the people began to understand who I was and why I was there, they were incredibly receptive to my cause and leaned forward to help. I traveled a long way to show that I cared about the people of Israel.

The next day, we arrived at the prime minister's office in Tel Aviv. Jewel spoke in Hebrew on my behalf to the security personnel and informed them of the purpose of my visit. I gave them a glimpse of *The Child* painting, and they loved it. After a short wait, Jewel went into the prime minister's office first, and then I was invited in. Jewel introduced me and announced that I was presenting a gift to the children of Israel.

When I met Prime Minister Shamir, I knew I was in the presence of greatness. I was brief, courteous, and most of all respectful and humble. I presented the painting to Prime Minister Shamir and told him why I was taking the painting around the world on a tour of peace. "Prime Minister Shamir, this painting is a way of saying thank you for working toward peace. This painting is for the children of Israel."

Prime Minister Shamir contemplated and gazed upon the painting, saying, "Yes, the children are in God's hand."

He commented on the children and their future. He spoke words of wisdom, like a sage grandfather. He was relaxed and warm, and I felt that he liked me as a person and was interested in what I was doing. In his presence, I was humbled by the teacher, soaking in his gracefulness. To me, his tone of voice impressed upon me that the people of Israel are people of love.

The meeting with Prime Minister Shamir in August 1988 was the beginning of a beautiful relationship with Israel and opened the doors for me to participate in the fortieth anniversary of Jewish statehood.

To commemorate the fortieth anniversary, the promoters planned a huge extravaganza concert at Masada near the Dead Sea. It was October 1988. Masada is an ancient fortification, and the site of a 73 AD battle in which the Jewish residents who lived atop the cliffs chose suicide rather than Roman enslavement. My dear friend and the concert's executive producer, Benny Boret, was part of the volunteer group producing the concert. He invited me as a special guest.

A private Mercedes Benz limousine escorted me across the scorching Israeli desert and to the concert site. We traveled for hours. As soon as I stepped out of the car, Benny embraced me like a brother. I carried with me five hundred letters and paintings from US children to present to the Israeli people. The children's letters were filled with expressions of love and peace. The people of Israel wept when they read the letters of love and support from elementary school children.

The people of Israel, especially the children, received the children's letters as precious gifts. The American children expressed a desire to connect as pen pals and to build relationships of peace with Israeli children. What a grand vision!

Evening drew near, and at dusk, torches lit the way for the guests arriving by car and bus. Nearly 4,000 people attended the concert. Security was tight due to the number of dignitaries who attended. The backdrop for the outdoor concert was the Dead Sea. To the right, along the mountain face, was the winding path to the top of the plateau, also lit with people holding torches. The design of the production was spectacular and full of color. The Israel Philharmonic Orchestra, led by Maestro Zubin Mehta, performed an extraordinary rendition of Mahler's Resurrection Symphony. One of the speakers proclaimed a profound message to the Jews in the Soviet Union, listening live by radio, and announced to the Soviet government, "Let my people go."

The fireworks at the end of the concert were an expression of exultation as the Israel national anthem played and the concert concluded. The next day, we returned to Masada for another ceremony that honored humanitarians who contributed to the welfare of Israel. The ceremony emcees presented each honoree with an Israeli flag neatly folded in a decorative box. The flags had been flown at Masada for the fortieth anniversary.

I was part of the audience and clapped for the honorees. Then, the emcee called the name "Danny Garcia." What was this? Was there another Danny Garcia in the audience?

I looked around to see what other Danny Garcia would step forward.

I said to myself, "Where is this other guy who has the same name as I have?"

The speaker called Danny Garcia again and stated that he is an American from the United States. I stood in shock, my legs trembling. I tried to keep my composure and willed my feet to move toward the stage. The closer I got to the platform, the more excited I became.

"Who am I?" I asked myself. "What are they going to do? What are they going to say?"

I reached the stage and approached the man making the presentations. It finally dawned on me that the gathering also honored me and had an Israeli flag for me too.

I accepted the gift. Once I received the flag, I felt like I was a part of the nation of Israel in body, mind, and spirit. Instinctively, I turned to face the audience, and with one motion lifted the flag out of its ornate box. Then I hoisted the corners of the flag with both arms as high as I could.

Facing the audience and exalting God, I shouted, "God bless Israel!"

The people erupted with cheers, jubilation, pride for their country, and tears. That day, I was as proud of the Israeli flag as I was of my own American flag. The flag represented their statehood and acknowledged their sovereignty as a country. I felt the love of Israel.

Benny told me that people often asked, "Who is the guy who raised the Israeli flag like that?"

After the ceremony, I met government officials and famous artists such as Gregory Peck, and Italian-French actor Yves Montand. I then returned to Jerusalem to continue my world tour. I traveled to Seoul, Korea, for the 1988 Summer Olympics and met the president of the Seoul Olympic Organizing Committee. I stayed with the Olympian contenders and attended the various events. While I was waiting for the games to begin in South Korea, I attended the church of Pastor David Yonggi Cho. At the time, his church was one of the largest in the world. American Pastor Robert Schuller was the guest speaker. I met and made a presentation to Pastor Cho, thanking him for his service to God. I then attended the opening ceremonies of the Olympic games and went back home to California.

President Reagan

Saying thank you is such a simple gesture. I thought even the most powerful people on earth appreciated this acknowledgment. I continued promoting *The Child* and made reproductions to present to world leaders and other known figures. Some of the recipients included Mother Theresa, Muhammed Ali, Redd Fox, Michael Jackson, and many others. Included in this list of honorees is President Ronald Reagan. He and Mrs. Reagan visited their home state of California on October 27, 1988, on a campaigning stop in San Diego. At the San Diego Sports Arena, I presented to his staff a framed reproduction of *The Child*. The President sent a gracious letter to me a few months later and expressed his thanks and commended my work. I cherish his letter dated December 2, 1988.

THE WHITE HOUSE

WASHINGTON

December 2, 1988

Dear Mr. Garcia:

Please accept my special thanks for the framed
reproduction of a segment of Mario Torero's
original mural, "The Child," which you presented
on the occasion of my recent visit to San Diego.
I want you to know that I truly appreciate your
kindness in sharing this symbolic work with me.
The children of the world are indeed our promise
for the future. I commend you for your dedication
in promoting a future of hope and peace.

With my best wishes,

Sincerely,

Ronald Reagan

Mr. Daniel Garcia
203 North Tremont
Oceanside, California 92054

Letter from President Ronald Reagan

Through my travels, I met and rubbed shoulders with remarkable people. When I returned to San Diego, though, I still needed to work and needed flexible hours. So, I returned to various law enforcement and security jobs to support my family. Sometimes I worked three jobs. I put my children into a Christian school and even worked security at their school. My relationship with God was continuing to deepen over the years.

My attention turned to children affected by poverty and war.

Bosnia

War raged in Europe, with ethnic and religious war in the Balkans from 1992–1995. I wanted to shine a light of hope for peace to the Bosnians, Croats, and Serbs. Although it was still a dangerous place, in January 1996, I went on a peace mission and took the fourteen-by-forty-eight-foot mural of *The Child,* this time on canvas, to the Bosnian theater. "NY Mike," who at the time owned San Diego Harley-Davidson, sponsored the trip and accompanied me to Bosnia and Herzegovina. Friends asked us to reconsider, but I felt that God was calling me to go.

Our intention was to share *The Child* as a sign of hope for the NATO troops in these countries—especially the US component, Task Force Eagle (1st Armored Division, V Corps). We also brought letters from US children to share with the children affected by the war. The city of Tuzla, one of the UN regional headquarters sites, is where I planned to have the mural exhibited. Tuzla was the headquarters of the US forces for the Multinational Division (MND) during Operation Joint Endeavor.

After we presented *The Child* to the US Embassy in Bosnia, we attempted to fly to Tuzla, but the plane had limited passenger seats. The crew had to bump the wives of ambassadors. They did agree, however, to take the canvas and the letters to Tuzla. After

The Child was put on a plane, the path of delivery was diverted. I received word from the CO of Task Force Eagle that the mural arrived in Zagreb, Croatia, and was on its way to the troops. Unfortunately, when I attempted to recover the mural after the exhibition, I was told it was lost. It has never been recovered.

Mike and I returned to the States, and I went back to work to support my family. However, the serious rifts in my marriage, which had been brewing for years, finally came to a head.

Betrayal

When I accepted Jesus, I became a totally new person with different values: I wasn't into money, fame, drugs, and the jet-setting life I had before. I did not want to do wrong. The former Danny Garcia (player, womanizer, drug user, and dealer) was fading away. I was into God, not material things. I wasn't the same person my wife married.

"You love God more than you love me," my wife told me.

"Don't you?" I responded. "Shouldn't you love God more than you love me?"

The huge gap in how we viewed God had expanded to a chasm. She was looking for someone to satisfy her needs, and that was no longer me. Stinging betrayal would strike once more as she left with another man. Amidst this ordeal, I heard a voice.

"Let it go," said the voice softly.

It was like a needle that punctured my balloon and released my hurt.

It was over. I had to get out of town.

The end of my second marriage was an emotional and spiritual kind of death. I was crushed, stabbed in the heart. I left her everything, taking nothing but the clothes on my back.

Anguished, I got into my car and started driving south on Interstate 5. As I approached the off-ramp to the San Diego Airport, my mind told me to accelerate and kill myself. What did I have left to live for? Could my life really be worth it? As I stepped on the gas, I heard a second voice call out.

"Please, pull over and park the car."

I obeyed that voice and found a payphone booth. I dialed an old friend and pastor in Bend, Oregon. I shared my story with my friend, and he asked me to get on the next bus north to Oregon. My friend ran a shelter for homeless and alcohol- and drug-addicted men. We lived simply with no phones and plenty of time to absorb nature. There was frequent daily prayer and emotional comfort through the Word of God. I received support and made new friends. After a few weeks, I felt emotionally able to return to Oceanside, California. A detective friend, Chris McDonough, took me in for a few days. But I was still distressed, near suicidal. As I slept on my friend's floor and instinctively rolled over to reach for my wife, I realized she wasn't there and panicked.

"Where are you?" I whispered.

Blinking in the dark, slowly recognizing that I was on the floor, not in my bed, I found myself *alone* and disoriented. She was not there. She would never be there again. This was my wake-up call. It was November 1996.

I kept beating myself up and replaying the events. Did everyone except me see the end coming as I denied what was so apparent? The community observed from afar that I was in my own refining crucible of life, being tried and refined. Could I take the heat of the furnace, or would I be consumed by the fire and die?

I thought this second marriage betrayal was the end of my life. Why go on? Go on for what? The fourteen years of marriage destroyed me, and I felt dead. Thoughts of suicide, rejection, and hopelessness returned with a fury. I had nothing left and nothing to live for.

"God, you know, if you're really out there, I need your help," I prayed. "I don't want to live anymore. Since you're the giver of life, I need you to give me life."

It was not the end. Letting go and letting God was the beginning. God alone had set me free. While I was in grief and despair, I would learn to appreciate the blessing. It was God's perfect will for my life.

CHAPTER 8:

"God, Give Me Life"— Emerging from the Crucible

As the year 1996 was coming to a close, it was difficult for me to see a new beginning at the end of my second marriage. The betrayal threw me into a crucible where I felt crushed and hopeless. I like the definition of *crucible*: "a place or situation in which people or ideas are tested severely, often creating something new or exciting in the process"

"God, you have to show me you are real. Please, give me life," I pleaded.

What was left of my life? Friends, coworkers, acquaintances, church folk, and neighbors were aware of the breakup and were sympathetic. I knew thousands of people due to my years of community outreach, but during my time of devastation, people were strangely distant. Friends' homes opened to me for short stints. I lingered in San Diego and realized I could not remain there. At the lowest point of my life, suffocating from depression, I knew it was time to go.

I'm Walking

"I'm leaving," I declared. "The way I feel now, I don't care if I live or die. I am going to walk and keep walking until God tells me to stop or heals me, or I wither and die."

Most people who heard this thought I had lost it, lost my mind. They asked, "You are just going to walk? Walk where?"

"Where are you going and how will you get there?" asked others.

"Who's going to help?"

"How can you do that? Are you sure?"

"Is God really telling you to walk? To just walk with no money, food, and clothes?"

"That's impossible, you can't do that."

Other people just ignored me. They did not want to be involved with my personal problems, and it was too strange, foreign, and incomprehensible to "just walk." I was such a popular guy, recognized in the community. Now, in my time of need, people disappeared, disassociated themselves from me. Some talked behind my back. Some blasted and criticized me.

"What's wrong with you? Are you crazy?"

"We love you, Danny, but you can't let what's going on with your wife destroy you. Don't do this. You aren't thinking right."

I was not crazy, and not insane. I was committed. God laid a path for me to plow *through* my pain. Suicidal thoughts plagued me. I felt rejected with no purpose. I felt like a failure. Loneliness crept in, and I kept hearing the words of those who doubted me. I was a fifty-one-year-old man who lost everything. I was emotionally numb; I felt dead inside.

Despite the emotions, my faith was still intact. I believed God was with me in my sorrow. It was time for a change of scenery, away from San Diego. A friend of a friend suggested San Francisco as my destination.

The next day, I boarded a plane from San Diego to San Francisco to stay with another friend who was in the film industry. Wrestling with my emotions, I needed to release the anger and painful rejection. Together, my friend and I came up with the idea of a walk beginning at Planet Hollywood.

Planet Hollywood arranged and held a small ceremony and launched my walk. I cut a ribbon, then started walking while my friend drove an escort vehicle and filmed the walk. My friend followed on foot for a few hours, then had to return home. I continued walking from San Francisco back to San Diego with hundreds of miles before me.

I started on December 7, 1996, the anniversary of a day which would live in infamy: Pearl Harbor Day.

Walking along California Highway 101, I was oblivious to the unrelenting rain and determined to keep walking. Even along the treacherous Dead Man's Curve—two narrow lanes with little visibility—I walked, even though drivers could not see me along the sharp curves. Trucks blasted dangerously close by and splashed rain all over me. The wind from the vehicles speeding by almost knocked me off the road. I realized that path was too dangerous, so I turned around and walked back down the road to the nearest city.

"I'm tired, I'm wet and cold, I'm hungry. I have to find a place to stay," I thought.

Half Moon Bay

That first day, on the verge of exhaustion, I had walked for eleven hours and found myself outside of the Half Moon Bay Inn, about fifty miles from Planet Hollywood. I thumbed through the mere forty-eight dollars in my pocket and wondered how I was going to pay for a room. I walked into the hotel, dripping wet, and explained to the general manager that I was walking from San Francisco to San Diego.

"I only have forty-eight dollars," I explained. Then I pulled out my money, soaked and soggy.

As I thought about what to say next, I remembered my friend NY Mike (the same Mike who accompanied me on the peace mission to Bosnia). Mike was a Vietnam veteran who served with the 101st Airborne Division. If I ever needed help, he told me that all I had to do was call him at the number on his business card. I explained my situation to the manager, and he let me call Mike. I told Mike what I was doing, then Mike asked to speak with the owner who was standing by and had overheard the entire story. Mike offered his credit card information to the owner to cover lodging and food for me. But the general manager, moved by my story, intervened.

"Your money is no good here," said the big-hearted manager. "You can stay here for as long as you need to."

The Half Moon Bay Inn gave me free room and board. I enjoyed their best luxury suite free of charge and stayed in Half Moon Bay for four days.

During the time that I was at Half Moon Bay Inn, another concerned, dear friend had heard of the separation from my wife and family, my departure from San Diego, and my walk. She was aware of my state of mind and was worried about me walking down the highway. My friend contacted my Marines in San Diego.

"One of your own is in trouble and needs help," she advised the Marines. She explained that I was walking alone on Highway 1 from San Francisco to San Diego for children.

"Ma'am, tell Danny to stay put until we arrive," the Marines instructed.

Marines do not leave fellow Marines stranded. Two motorbikes and a few Humvees showed up at my hotel door. The Humvees were light military trucks, four-wheel-drive vehicles. The Marine Corps Reserve Unit from San Diego followed me as my escort, covering my front and back the entire way to San Diego. They protected me.

For the first time in a very long time, with the arrival of the Marines, the cloud of darkness broke. Light overwhelmed me: I was not alone. I had my brothers. Help from my USMC family, NY Mike, the general manager of Half Moon Bay Inn, and, mostly, help from God, reassured me that I could go on and could finish this walk.

In my mind, I thought I would walk to bring attention to the needs of children all over the world.

My goal was fifty miles a day, eight to ten hours of walking, at a pace of about five miles an hour. Although my body ached, I did not quit. At times, my mind transported me into another zone. I looked to my left and saw an image of myself, outside of my body, walking next to me. Then, I turned to my right and saw my Marine buddy next to me, Marines covering my front, side, and back: Semper Fidelis, always faithful. Every night, hotels provided complimentary rooms for our stay. I encountered the favor of God and His provision for my every need.

The first night we checked into the hotel, there were five or six of us in one room. One guy snored so loudly that, while he was sleeping, the other guys picked up his cot, opened the patio door, and put him outside. When he woke and found himself outside, he simply went and slept in one of the Humvees.

Every fifty miles, a new set of Marine Reservists relieved their comrades and assumed vehicle escort until we reached San Diego. The Marines defined my route and, when necessary, detoured me to avoid mudslides, dangerous roads, and congested traffic. It was a grueling walk of five hundred miles—a bit more considering the detours. Although I had done some walks before, five hundred miles in less than two weeks was my first walk of endurance on a major highway.

Mental Discipline

Questions I have often answered are: What happens to your body when you walk fifty miles a day? How do you walk fifty miles?

For the first three miles of this walk, I mentally prepared. My body had to catch up with what my mind was telling me. I calculated my desired distance and pace. If I walked at five miles an hour, then walked for eight hours, that equated to forty miles. Physically, I picked up the pace to five miles an hour and timed myself with a watch or with the escort vehicle's speedometer. When I was behind, the Marines told me to pick up my speed. The Marines developed the structure of my walk, like a military exercise. They were an organized, committed, and focused team.

I welcomed the refreshing breezes and overcast chilly mornings because this weather cooled my body and helped me remain focused. At the fifteen-to-twenty-mile mark, my fingers and toes started to swell. The more mileage walked, the more I experienced inflammation and loss of circulation. If I sensed a muscle cramp in my calf, I ran to break the cycle and to stop the cramping. As I approached the thirty-five-to-forty-mile mark, my whole body was in trauma. I told myself not to quit and that I only had a few more miles to go for that day.

My eyes took photographs, step by step. When driving in a car, it is easy to miss details of the landscape. But when walking, I saw more houses, farms, and children. On a freeway, the semi-trucks presented the most danger, zooming by at sixty-to-seventy miles per hour. The turbulence in the wake of the trucks was so forceful that it blew and knocked me off the road. I mentally prepared and physically braced myself for the blast. Walking like this was as much a mental challenge as it was a physical challenge. It was an athletic undertaking.

San Diego and the Mexican Border

When I reached the destination of San Diego, my Marine Corps escorts embraced me. They saw me to the end of the five-hundred-mile walk and shared the victory.

"Semper Fi," my brothers said as they bid me farewell and Godspeed.

Officials of the City of San Diego greeted me, as did the media. A friend of mine assumed coordination of the next portion of the walk: from the California border to Tijuana. He explained that there was a special activity taking place to provide a Christmas to kids who have no money and no gifts. He invited me to a "Dia de Los Ninos" (Day of the Children) Celebration at the Caliente Racetrack in Tijuana, Mexico. McDonald's sponsored the event so kids could attend the yearly festival.

It was a short walk—about an hour—to cross the border. Mexican immigration officials expected me and told me to wait for an official escort. Less than an hour later, I heard the thunder of dozens of motorcycles approaching. As I walked, I noticed all the police motorcycles riding by and going in a circle.

"Is the president of Mexico going to be here?" I asked my friend. "Someone important must be coming."

He said, "No, Danny, they are here for you."

Wow, I was shocked. Who was I? Just a nobody, I thought. Through the Mexican media, the people heard that a man walking from San Francisco was coming to see them. My motorcycle escorts positioned themselves around me as I walked in the rain to the Caliente Racetrack. As we came closer to the entrance of the stadium, the whole convoy turned on their sirens at once, causing a thunderous roar. All the police motorcycles entered Caliente in a procession, tagged along behind me and filing in, one by one, forming several long rows. The rain continued to pour.

Upon my arrival, and to my complete surprise, I saw a completely full stadium. About 20,000 children of all ages were waiting for me! All these people looked forward to my arrival and honored me with their presence. When I saw the children, their joy, innocence, and exuberance melted my heart.

One of the officials spoke to me in Spanish, saying, "Please tell our children what you are doing because they need to know there are people in this world who deeply care about them."

The first words out of my mouth were "Yo les amo [I love you]."

"¡Viva Dios y viva los niños! ["Long live God and long live the children!"] ¡Viva Dios y viva los niños! ¡Viva Dios y viva los niños!" I chanted.

The children went wild and joined me in unison. In Spanish, I thanked the children and told them I was humbled and honored to be at the Day of the Children celebration with them. I explained my walk and that I was almost hit by trucks several times, soaked by the rain, and had to take a detour because of a mudslide. Fifty miles a day, eight-to-eleven hours a day, took a toll on my body. I told them that my fingers and toes swelled, that my back felt like it was breaking and that my mind told me to quit.

"Don't give up; don't quit no matter how difficult your task. God is with you. I love you, and I am walking for you."

The stadium burst into clapping and a roar of praise and joy. In return, the children shouted, "Viva Danny Garcia!" I was touched, humbled, and amazed.

His outpouring of love continued to surround me. I experienced overwhelming gratitude. I received the giving spirit from people who materially have so little but, out of the abundance of their hearts, give so much. The children of Tijuana confirmed my purpose: I would walk for children. My walk of love and healing began. I never looked back.

Walk to Forgive, Walk to Heal

I stayed committed to walking for children. The old Danny Garcia was concentrating on his past life and what had been lost. The new Danny Garcia was a man walking for children and for Jesus. God called me to walk through pain, to sacrifice for others, and to love people. God used walking to answer my prayers and to give me a new life. More so, He healed my broken heart through the love of people I met along my walk. With each step, God chipped away the unforgiveness and anger. I also forgave myself for the bad decisions I had made and the people I had hurt along the way. My attitude was to forgive and move forward.

You don't want to miss this!

The essence of my walks is to display *the power of the Love of God.*

You see, when I asked God to give me life, I needed to connect with Him and know that He would connect with me. That connection came when others, who saw me hurting and walking out my pain, graciously extended love to me. I experienced love through acts of kindness. People along the way showed compassion and concern. My Marine brothers protected and supported me. Total strangers extended hospitality and encouragement. God sent people to *love me* every step of the way.

The power of love had contagious effects. As I received, I, in turn, gave love, watched love blossom, and witnessed how love conquers all. As only the Almighty can do, Jesus revealed His love to me and through me during this walk.

The gift of love healed me.

As I received, Jesus expanded my heart with the capacity to love people unconditionally. The love of Jesus healed me, continued through me, and enabled me to touch others with a smile, a gesture, a handshake, and with prayer.

From a dead man walking, I was transformed. I had my mission, one that God uniquely qualified and prepared me to do: to walk and pray, to share the love of Jesus with all I met.

Part II

Introduction

As you are reading this introduction, you are one of the thousands of people all over the world who have been waiting for this book. I have shared my life with the poorest of the poor and the rich and famous. They ask, "When are you going to write your book? I'll buy it. I'll read it!"

Maybe you skipped to Part II and want to jump right into reading about my walks. I'd like to suggest not skipping Part I of this book so that you can understand why a man would want to walk all over the world. What would drive such a crazy idea? What would sustain me and compel me consistently for over twenty-two years of walking?

Part I of this book talks about the source of my passion and my calling. Men and women of greatness, success, fame, and notoriety (what you can see) have suffered, sacrificed, toiled in their own lives—even failed countless times. It may be years, decades, or centuries before others recognize their achievements. Some of those achievements are not recognized during their lifetimes, but many years afterward. I wanted to write this book while I am still alive and with my own words.

Have you heard the phrase "WWJD" or "What would Jesus do?" The phrase became popular and "WWJD" beaded letters were made into bracelets, necklaces, etc. to get people to think (and maybe act) like Jesus. For me, it wasn't as much "What *would* Jesus do?" but "What *did* Jesus do?"

Jesus walked. Jesus prayed. Jesus preached, taught, sacrificed. Jesus loved. I wanted to be like Jesus, so I would walk, pray, teach, and sacrifice. I love you.

Every walk I've done is different. In the beginning, I physically walked each mile and, with the help of my support and escort vehicles, could measure the mileage. Over time, the purpose, the territory, and the people reached would be much more important than counting how many miles I walked. Inclement weather, formidable terrain, and physically dangerous situations (*survival* for your life) are at the forefront, and counting miles fades to insignificance. In truth, considering practice walks, casual walking for errands, detours, and working out, I will say I've walked more than advertised. The number of miles is not a badge of honor. It is the children and the people who are important.

Am I walking for a world record? For fame? For a title? For money?

No, I am not. I am not running for office, and I don't want a political position. I have been asked to lead churches and to consider being an ambassador, a talent agent, and the mayor of Bronx, New York. I only want Jesus.

Every walk I've done is challenging. Think about the different countries, cultures, languages, and socio-economic conditions. Think about peaceful nations versus war-torn areas. Some countries are hinged on fragile peace agreements, and social unrest could blow up into violence at any time (think of the Middle East and Africa). Some countries suffer from the wrath of nature through earthquakes, fire, drought, and floods. Then there are the afflictions from mankind: bombings, genocidal slayings, and ideological religious divides which have spawned barbaric groups who believe they are killing "for God."

I've been to some of these places—dangerous places—where children suffer and die. Which leads me to how every walk is similar with a central purpose: to walk and pray for children and world peace. Make no mistake; I love my job (although I did not ask for it—God called me). My goal, in all humility, is to be an imitator of Christ.

So I walk, I pray, I teach, I sacrifice, and principally, I seek to love.

Part II of this book describes my initial walks. I am thankful for the journalists who captured moments and memories and for the media (interviews, video recordings, newscasts). The articles and photographs have helped me and my wife piece together over twenty-two years of walking across the globe and to chronicle the journey of "The Walking Man" emerging from the crucible.

CHAPTER 9:

First 3,500 Miles Plus, Walks in the US

Discovering the healing in walking, I was invigorated and eager to keep going and walking across America.

After Tijuana, I returned to San Diego to prepare for the rest of this inaugural walk: first Alexandria, Louisiana, to Oklahoma City, Oklahoma; then Miami, Florida, to New York City, New York. Part I describes the first segment from San Francisco, California, to Tijuana, Mexico. This walk was not a straight walk across the United States. I broke up the walk locations because I wanted the support of my Marine Corps brothers along the way.

Domestic Bombings Shake the Nation

During the mid-1990s, as I was being refined in the fire, America was also being tried in fire. Our country began to experience terrorism domestically and on foreign soil through bombings targeted at symbols of the American government. New York City's World Trade Center was the target of terrorists in 1993; six were killed and over a thousand injured. A new terrorist figure, Osama Bin Laden, emerged. He applauded a June 1996 truck bombing of the Khobar Towers housing complex in Saudi Arabia. That bombing killed nineteen US American service members and wounded nearly five hundred. This same Bin Laden warned of more acts of violence to come, foreshadowing the September 11, 2001 attacks in New York City.

Bombings du jour—more and more sensational—were fueled by religious beliefs and executed by suicide bombings. As a nation of people who value human life, we struggled to comprehend suicide bombers. How is there honor and reward in suicidal death?

On our home turf, a massive domestic bombing rocked Oklahoma City on April 19, 1995. What shook the nation as strongly as the destructive blast was the senseless loss of children's lives. The blast ripped through multiple stories of the Alfred P. Murrah Federal Building, including the daycare center. The explosion injured six hundred fifty people and claimed the lives of one-hundred-sixty-eight souls, including nineteen young children.

The carnage from the bombing and the loss of human life, especially the children, profoundly touched me. I prayed, "God, help me walk for these children, and all children across the world; protect me every step of the way."

He would not let me down, and God honored this prayer through dangers, toils, and trials. Before I started walking in 1996, I traveled to Oklahoma City just after the bombing in April 1995 and had *The Child* mural displayed at the Myriad Convention Center to bring hope to the city.

"Every time I see an act of hatred, violence, or terrorism where a child is a victim or is injured," I said, "it tears at my heart."

Later, in 1997, my church in San Diego bought me a plane ticket back to Louisiana for a walk in tribute to the attack. I stopped in New Orleans first to coordinate support with the Marine Corps Reserves. From there, I went to Alexandria, Louisiana, where a Pentecostal church provided for my needs as I planned the seven hundred miles from Alexandria to Oklahoma City. The walk was a tribute to the many victims of the bombing, and especially the innocent children who lost their lives through a senseless act of terrorism.

I began the second segment of this walk on my birthday, March 18, 1997, with the goal to reach Oklahoma City on April 19th, 1997—the second anniversary of the Oklahoma City bombing.

"Why walk and start from Louisiana?" the reporters wanted to know.

That's where the Marines were. From Bossier City, Louisiana, the 23rd Marine Reserve Unit, B Company, First Battalion, provided a three-man escort and a van to follow me. They had my back, and some of them walked with me along Interstate 20. Always faithful, the Marines not only believed in my cause but believed in me, as a Marine.

The Marines were organized and knew how to plan a route, block traffic, and protect me from being hit. They took care of all the walk logistics and were incredibly mission-focused.

I was also asked by reporters, "How do you get so much free publicity?"

If you have a compelling story, God provides the public relations, and the story will be told. In Marshall, Texas, the local Holiday Inn provided me a room where I stayed for the night and was interviewed by the Marshall News Messenger. The media continued supportive coverage of my walk as I passed through Louisiana and Texas and on to my destination of Oklahoma City.

I told the newspapers, "I choose to really do something to try to resolve some of the problems that are going on with the children in our world today. We must act instead of talk. I've made a decision to act."

Some also asked, "How do you walk without any money?"

God supplied through friends, supporters, and sponsors. In addition to the US Marines and US Army Reserves, hotels gave me complimentary stays. The Brooks shoe company supplied two pairs of sneakers, and a man named Manny Grey donated a telephone calling card. A nutrition company and an essential oils company provided health products to fuel my walk. For this walk, a dear friend, Jennifer Dixon of Temecula, helped with coordinating support from California, Texas, and Oklahoma. I am deeply grateful to Jennifer for her support and love.

The Unexpected, A Day in the Life

Just north of Dallas-Ft Worth, in Denton, Texas, I connected with Marines from the 2nd Battalion, 14th Regiment. They escorted me with a Humvee from Fort Worth to Gainesville, Texas, near the Oklahoma border. Major Pete Ahern told the media that he and his men wanted to meet me and help me in any way because I was a former Marine.

"Once a Marine, always a Marine," said the major.

Walking north on the shoulder of Interstate 35 clearly stands out as an unexpected "day in the life." One of my Marine escorts (Don Droddy) wanted to walk with me to see what it is like on the road. He accompanied me for about thirty miles on this walk. Sgt Jesse Molina drove the Humvee behind us. It rained that whole day, and we were beat. The interstates are dangerous with cars speeding by. Any lapse or moment of inattention could end your life. And so it was that day. Add adverse weather, such as hail. We kept walking in the hail, crazy as that sounds.

Suddenly, on the other side of Interstate 35, to my left, something jolted me from my state of focus. I heard shrieking tires, shattering glass, and smashing metal. It was a two-car vehicle crash.

I stopped, turned my head over my right shoulder, and instructed my team, "Pull over to the side and stay here."

As I ran toward the crash, I jumped over the interstate barrier and rushed to the scene. A young woman and a child were trapped in one of the cars. Under the hood of the wrecked car, a fire had erupted. Smoke was billowing from under the hood and began to seep into the car. I tried to open the driver's side door—it was jammed. I looked into the woman's eyes, and she was clearly frightened and panicked. There was no time for words, only action. The car could have exploded at any moment.

I kept yanking on the door with both hands, and it finally dislodged. By this time, one of the Marines had arrived at my side, and as the door flung open, the woman thrust a small child into my arms. I quickly handed the child to my fellow Marine.

"Here, take the child to another vehicle, out of the hail," I shouted.

The woman reached up, and I grabbed her arms and pulled her out of the car. She was coughing, catching her breath, and searching frantically for the child. We ushered her to the safe vehicle, and she only had a moment to say, "Thank you." She disappeared and took shelter in the car with the child.

In the confusion, with hail pelting my body, I began directing traffic around the crash. Then Texas state troopers arrived on the scene and took over. With the grace of God and His supernatural favor, we saved two lives. Once the troopers took over and we knew the two were safe, we jumped back over the interstate and kept walking from Denton to Sanger, Texas.

"Sergeant," I encouraged the young Marine, "it's another day in the life of Danny Garcia. Every day is an adventure."

When we approached Sanger, Texas, a young man stopped and wanted to buy me lunch.

"I'm not asking for money," I said.

"I know, I just want to buy you lunch," the young man replied.

And that's how it has been for all my walks. Sometimes people honked their horns and waved in support when they drove by. God moved the hearts of people, and all my needs were met through the generosity of others. People wanted to help! They wanted to be part of something bigger than themselves and genuinely wanted to participate, even if they couldn't walk the steps with me.

Approaching the Oklahoma border and having walked twenty-five-to-fifty miles a day, my legs ached with pain. I had put braces on my legs for support. At night, I rubbed essential oils into my muscles and then packed both legs with ice to reduce swelling. I had to take care of my body and be ready for the next day of walking.

When I arrived in Oklahoma City, I asked that a few people join me for the last mile into the city and to the bombing site. To my amazement, on April 19, 1997, firefighters and police greeted me and escorted me in. The firefighters presented me with a cement block from the destroyed building, and I held it tenderly. I felt like I was holding all of Oklahoma City in my hands.

A local newspaper wrote an article, and staff writer Diane Hazel quoted me: "I'm walking in memory of the children that were killed and to lift the spirits of the children left behind."

The Oklahoma City bombing shattered not only Oklahoma City but the entire nation. The walk was also a walk of prayer for all who died, for the families hurt by the murder of so many innocent souls. And yet, from the rubble, we become stronger as a nation.

New York-Bound, Through a Tornado

New York City: the next destination and the third leg of the journey. I decided to start in Florida and walk up the eastern coast. I bent my head and asked God for his assurance and guidance: "Lord, am I walking the way you want me to walk? Am I living the way you want me to live?"

God had called me to walk and pray for our children. I was to walk by faith and not by sight.

I left Miami, Florida, on May 11, 1997, (Mother's Day) and journeyed to New York City, a 1,500-mile trek. My plan was to be there by the 4th of July (less than two months). For this leg of the walk, I did not have a Marine Corps escort. I was alone and unafraid, pounding the pavement and headed into Florida sand, swamp, and heat.

Reporters interviewed me as I walked across the famous Bridge of Lions in St. Augustine and headed to Jacksonville. I told them, "I want them [the children] to know that I love them and that the Lord loves them."

"Now, you be careful, Danny," the locals warned. "On that road, you have alligators on one side and water on the other side. And the gators like to cross the road from time to time. You be careful now."

A newspaper article described how I looked: I wore a blue headband, multi-colored fluorescent headphones, and knee pads. I threw a backpack over my shoulder, grabbed my walking stick, and took off walking. I traveled light and carried an extra pair of shoes. When I walked, I focused on my breathing and listened to

God. A certain rhythm took over: inhale, exhale, and step—one foot in front of the other. I either gazed ahead or at the ground. This was time with my Lord and, as I was silent, he began to talk to me profoundly.

Florida's weather can change quickly from sunny to stormy. And so it was this day. Strangely, I saw no people on the road, no houses in sight. There was an eerie calm. Gray clouds enveloped the daylight, and the clouds began to change to a darker, ominous color. Something was happening, and it was happening quickly. What was this?

Tornado!

My thoughts raced, "What if I get stranded? I have no escort, no one knows I am here, and I have no shelter. I have to get outta here!"

Rain came next and then gusts of strong wind; strong enough to knock me back three steps for every one step I struggled to take forward. I popped my head up and blinked hard to squeeze out the rain in my eyes. Then I saw it, coming toward me from my left at ten o'clock: a dark, swirling cloud . . . the tornado funnel. The tornado plucked telephone poles like toothpicks and threw them in the air. Whatever wasn't tied down was sucked into the funnel, and I even saw cattle thrown around like flecks in the churning cloud.

"Lord, help me," I urgently prayed. Then I started running, literally running for my life.

I had to find shelter. In the maelstrom of wind and debris, I caught a glimpse of a sign barely dangling to its post and whipping about like a flimsy piece of paper. I knew this was a sign from God—I had seen *nothing* on that road before. I told myself that maybe I could find shelter there. As I drew nearer, I could see the sign was for a restaurant and pool hall. I bolted as fast as I could to escape the funnel.

When I reached the door, I rushed in and quickly slammed the door behind me. With a gasp of relief, I was thankful to be out of the tornado's path. I was a mess: out of breath, completely soaked, and covered head to toe with dirt that the wind gusts had slapped upon me.

I sighed deeply and then noticed the silence. It was like Gary Cooper in a scene from the movie *High Noon* or better, the movie *Tombstone*. I was like one of the gunslingers who burst into the saloon, then pauses and looks around, hearing only the sound of the swinging doors behind him. The restaurant was dead silent inside, I could hear only my own breathing. All eyes were on me. Outside, croaking frogs (what seemed like an invasion of thousands), belted loudly. I straightened myself, swiped the dripping water off my face, and walked slowly to the bar. All eyes followed me.

"Can I get you something to drink?" The bartender broke the thickness and the intensity and gave me a sign that I was welcome, praise God.

I sputtered, "Can I have some water?"

"Sure," said the bartender, a bit confounded. "Tell me, are you OK? Why were you out there? Where's your car? Why are you walking?" I began to tell the owners about my walk from Miami to New York. I asked if there were any Marine units close by, but there were none in those parts.

"Would you like to use our bathroom? Would you like to shower?"

"Yes, I would. That would be nice." I was grateful for the shelter, water, and a chance to wash the dirt and grime off me.

"You know, you can't leave now. You have to stay for a while until the storm passes."

I was stuck, and so were all the patrons of the restaurant; confined by mother nature until the tornado passed. As I recounted my saga, more people came over to listen, enthralled. They were interested and supportive, and like so many I encountered, they wanted to help me. When I told them that I was walking for children from Miami to New York City, they gave me a tall glass of water, a meal, and a hotel for the night. After the storm subsided, the owners took me to a hotel about a thirty-minute drive from the restaurant which had become a tornado refuge.

"Take care of him. We're paying for the bill; he'll stay overnight."

I bid these beautiful people farewell and thanked them and my Lord Jesus for watching over me and carrying me through the tornado. I give glory to God for saving me from the path of that tornado. Kindness and hospitality from the hands of strangers, yet warmly familiar and cozy, became a hallmark of my walks.

"Just another day in the life of Danny Garcia," I mused.

Aside from the tornado, Florida weather can also be stifling in its heat and humidity. With humidity came tiny biting insects, and they were attracted to me. From St. Augustine to Jacksonville, I was parched and swarmed by sand fleas. From Jacksonville, I detoured my route to Georgia. In Atlanta, I visited the headquarters of Holiday Inn to thank them for supporting me. The hotels were all franchises, so the owners, out of kindness, would provide me with food and places to sleep.

Don't Ever Quit

Seeing a man walking is a curious sight. Where is he going? Why is he walking on the highway? Will he just get out of the way? Why won't he use the sidewalk?

Well, my walking was not a casual stroll. I was on a mission to encourage children to not give up. Walking and praying had become my mission from God, and I knew Jesus was with me.

As I made my way up the Eastern Seaboard, I arrived at Marine Corps Base Quantico—headquarters of the extraordinary United States Marine Corps. Quantico news wrote about an inherent quality of Marines: the "urge to continue to excel [which] burns inside them, the urge which tells you to never quit." This was my message to children—to not give up.

About this time, I received a great letter from my former commanding officer who had been promoted to four-star general and the commandant of the Marine Corps: General Krulak.

His handwritten note read: "You always had your eye on making the world a better place . . . you are *doing* it!"

26 June 1997

Dear Mr. Garcia,

Congratulations on your awesome accomplishment! I cannot tell you how moved I was when I heard about what you are doing to help the children. Many of our children are in desperate circumstances, and your "Walk Across America" is bringing their cries for help to the attention of our communities. I am very proud of your many accomplishments; from establishing the nonprofit organization, "Children of our World," to your many other walks for children. You have served as an inspiration to us all ... and motivated many to take notice of our children's plight and help recognize and fulfill their needs.

With every step you take, you do our nation proud. You have taken an active role in changing our world for the better, and I, and our entire Corps of Marines, salute you! Thank you for helping the children of our world to have a brighter future. They deserve it!

Sincerely,

C. C. KRULAK
General, U.S. Marine Corps
Commandant of the Marine Corps

You always had your eye set on making a better world... you are doing it!

Letter from General C.C. Krulak, Commandant, US Marine Corps

President Clinton

So, picking up this story from Quantico, Virginia, the next stop was our nation's capital. Passing through Washington, D.C., I offered my walking stick and a videotape to then-president Bill Clinton to thank him. President Clinton injured his knee in March 1997 at the home of pro golfer Greg Norman in Florida. During his recovery, I thought he would appreciate my walking stick. Although I did not personally meet him, I left my gifts with the White House staff and kept walking northward. Unbeknownst to me, President Clinton received my gift and wanted to talk to me! So the president of the United States called my church in San Diego, but I wasn't there.

"Hello, I would like to speak to Danny Garcia. This is Bill Clinton."

"Yeah, and I'm the Queen of England," laughed the church secretary.

"Ma'am, this is Bill Clinton, the president," he politely insisted. "I would like to speak to your pastor."

The secretary got it this time, and when she did, she fell out of her chair. *The president of the United States was on the line.* She scrambled and ran to get Pastor Larson. Pastor Larson took the call and later told me that he had a wonderful conversation with Mr. Clinton. The President wanted, on behalf of himself and Mrs. Clinton, to thank me for the walking stick. President Clinton later wrote me a kind personal letter dated July 2, 1997, acknowledging the gift.

THE WHITE HOUSE
WASHINGTON

July 2, 1997

PERSONAL

Mr. Daniel Garcia
1765 Pentecost Way
San Diego, California 92105

Dear Danny,

Thank you so much for the walking stick
And the videotape. It was a pleasure to
receive these mementos of your special journey
From Miami to New York, and I appreciate your
Thoughtfulness.

Hillary and I are delighted to know about
efforts such as yours to increase awareness of
Children's needs and safety. We wish you every
future success.

Sincerely,

Bill Clinton

Letter from President Bill Clinton

I then traveled northwesterly toward Pennsylvania. By mid-June 1997, I made it to Northeast Philadelphia (Trevose, PA) and thankfully reunited with US Marines, the 3rd Battalion, 14th Marine Unit. After my close call with the tornado in Florida, I was overjoyed to have disciplined and squared-away Marines covering me again. I was given the grand tour and, like the "Italian Stallion" in the movie *Rocky*, I ran up the famous steps and looked over the city of Philadelphia, inspired to finish the journey. The Marines put me up in a Radisson hotel, where I was treated graciously. The escorts resumed with Marines and a Humvee, and this time teenagers from the local Young Marines joined part of the walk on US Route 1 toward New York. The mission-focused team coordinated all logistics, publicity, news, lodging, and food for the last leg.

USMC Tank Escort on Atlantic City Boardwalk

When I reached New Jersey, the Marines of USMC Recruiting Command, Recruiting Station New Jersey, surprised me. Instead of a Humvee, they greeted me with several tanks and escorted me to Atlantic City. On the boardwalk, I walked with the tanks tracking behind. We stopped traffic, and everyone moved aside to witness this show of force. The Marines told me that the Marine Corps commandant, Gen Krulak, had a speaking engagement at one of the hotels, so we proceeded down the boardwalk to find the commandant.

I walked in and said to the hotel staff, "My understanding is that General Krulak is speaking here. Can you please tell him he has visitors outside waiting for him?"

The Marines lined up in front of the hotel and stood in rank file. The tanks, barrels facing forward, lined up behind the troops. The Marines were ready to pay respect to their commandant.

When Gen Krulak came out of the hotel, he was pleasantly surprised that his Marines were there to meet him. Then he saw me.

"Sgt Garcia, what are you doing here?" he asked incredulously.

The commandant took the opportunity to inspect the troops and talk with them.

"Do you know who Sgt Garcia is? Do you know what he has done?"

I was floored when Gen Krulak praised my walk across America and spoke so eloquently of me. What a man, what a leader. I did not know how anyone could top a tank escort along the Atlantic City boardwalk. From there, I continued walking to New York City with a Marine vehicular escort followed by police cars flashing their lights.

New York City, my birthplace, was the final stop of the journey. If you know New Yorkers, they do everything *big*. New Year's Day, Madison Square Garden, and, of course, pizza. I could go on and on about the city that never sleeps. When one of their own is coming to town, New York City does it big. On July 2, 1997, I crossed over the George Washington Bridge from New Jersey to New York City (Public Affairs Office), but not walking. New York City did not allow foot traffic on this bridge. After 1,500 miles, the Marines would not let me walk.

"Danny, from here you ride," the Marines told me.

Then, they put me in a stretch limousine and drove me across the bridge. I stood and poked myself up through the limo roof. On the other side of the bridge, New York City greeted me with much fanfare and a large group of supporters, including a platoon of Marines, recruiters, and new recruits. A Navy chaplain in all-white gave the invocation for the welcome reception, and the media covered the story. Escorts were on every side, waving to me as I smiled and waved back. I loved New York. New York loved me back.

We drove to Harlem in a truck called a "deuce and a half." In Harlem, my stomping grounds, I was met by friends and by a fascinating lady: Queen Mother Dr. Delois Blakely, the community mayor of Harlem, the "Harlem Street Nun," and the original sister of the movie *Sister Act*. Then, we drove to the UN, where I completed the journey and did what I said I would do: walk from Miami to New York City.

Journalists have asked me, "So, Danny, why are you walking?"

"To show my love for the children of our world. I am bringing attention to children's rights and to let them know *someone* cares about them, no matter how bad things may seem."

The New York State Assembly awarded me a citation dated July 9, 1997, to commemorate my arrival in the Bronx.

A Latin newspaper also covered the story with an article titled "Por Amor a los Ninos," or "For the Love of the Children." One step at a time, covering approximately 3,500 miles, three segments, in seven months. I did it—what a sense of accomplishment.

What was next? I had an idea!

I asked myself, "What if I were to continue walking overseas to keep the cause for children alive, to spread love in other countries, to continue encouraging others as I had done with *The Child* mural in Bosnia? London, the real Queen of England, Prince Charles, Princess Diana, and the Royal Family—what would walking in Europe be like?"

Walking across the US wasn't so bad, so I decided to plan for walks in Europe. I went to New York City and met with a jeweler, Johnny Lu of LuCoral. Johnny knew I was going to England and that I needed a gift for Princess Diana. Then he showed me something fit for a princess. It was a large cross made of 8,000 pearls, set against a red velvet backing and framed. It must have been worth thousands of dollars. Johnny gave me the beautiful pearl cross to present as a gift.

A personal friend and TV producer, Mitch Rabin, also lived in New York City.

He said, "I will sponsor your trip to England if I can go."

Mitch wanted to film the tour, so he sponsored this trip and we left for London. When we arrived at our hotel, we had planned on meeting Princess Diana and presenting her with the cross. Tragically, the royal princess was killed in a car accident in Paris on August 31st, 1997. We were devastated and grieved along with the world at the loss of the "People's Princess." We canceled our presentation. I decided to reserve the pearl cross for another group as a gift of love. I believed that God would reveal to me who would receive the cross.

I returned to San Diego to revise my walking plans.

My critics called me crazy, but I was committed. I decided to continue on my path of walking. Despite potential dangers, the doubts of others, and the unknown circumstances ahead of me, I endured. Walking in the United States among my own American citizens was a start. I pressed on and knew I was not alone. I found strength because I was confident that Jesus was in my corner.

Super Bowl XXXII, Danny Garcia Day

I remember Super Bowl Sunday, January 25, 1998. For US football fans, the Super Bowl is one of the most anticipated sports events, for both the sport and the commercials. I decided to walk for the teams and athletes about to battle for the championship. The Green Bay Packers faced off against the Denver Broncos in Super Bowl XXXII.

That Sunday, I started early in the morning from Tijuana, Mexico, and walked to the Qualcomm (also known as Jack Murphy) Stadium, arriving early in the afternoon. Body Wise International (a health and nutrition company) was my sponsor. My dear friend Lorella Losa helped to organize the walk. Lorella was a spiritual mentor in my early days of ministry and saw me through many dark days.

"There is a great deal of power that goes around this man. People may not always understand where he is coming from, but they know somehow that he is different, and they respect him," said Lorella.

A Marine Corps color guard and a group of children met us, and we said a prayer for the athletes. The Denver Broncos won that Super Bowl, defeating the Green Bay Packers, 31–24. Although I was not spending much time in San Diego, I was humbled that the mayor of San Diego, Susan Golding, recognized my walks and work for children and proclaimed January 25, 1998, as "Danny Garcia Day."

Hoboken, Walk for "Blue Eyes"

In the summer of 1998, the world lost another great American figure, and I was deeply saddened. It was May 14, 1998, when Frank Sinatra died.

Frank Sinatra was an entertainment icon. Music had always been part of my life and walks, and I enjoyed all types of music, including the music of "Blue Eyes," Mr. Frank Sinatra.

When I heard that he had died, I knew I had to do a walk in his memory to say thank you and goodbye. On Fox News, I saw a man singing a song that he had written for Frank's eightieth birthday. (This man, Bruce Stephen Foster, would later write a thematic song for my walks).

Frank Sinatra was born in Hoboken, New Jersey, and that is where I decided to start walking, in the rain. I remember catching the flu and having a high temperature. But that wouldn't stop me. I would not quit. My stopping point would be Atlantic City and the Sands Hotel, the last place where Frank Sinatra performed live. As I got closer to Atlantic City, a car was zipping and dashing near the parking lot of the Sands Hotel. The driver turned sharply just a few feet in front of me and nearly hit me. A journalist, Martin DeAngelis, walked with me and witnessed the driver who almost sent me "into another world." Another close call, but by this time I had gotten used to cars almost hitting me. Another rule of walking: be alert and watch out.

"Frank gave a lot, and I liked the way he sang," I told the reporter. He did it his way, and for that I respected him.

King Hussein I of Jordan

After my stay in Atlantic City, I heard that King Hussein I of Jordan was ill from cancer. I wanted to do something. To this day, in my opinion, no other world leader was as loved and as respected as King Hussein I. He ruled for forty-six years and played a major historical role in peacemaking efforts in the Middle East. The king was loved, not only by his people but by people throughout the Middle East and by other heads of state.

I was told that the king was at the Mayo Clinic in the US. So, I wrote him a personal letter of encouragement, told him of my vision to walk for children and peace, and provided him with gifts as a get-well gesture. I expressed that I was praying for him, for his recovery from cancer, and that I cared for him.

The king wrote me a very kind letter dated August 20, 1998. It was full of grace and appreciation. Never doubt the power of a personal letter and words of kindness and love. The king, like any person undergoing cancer treatments, needed words of encouragement and support during this time. God used me to bring comfort to the king. I cherish his letter to this day.

August 30th, 1998

Dear Friend,

Thank you so much for your kind message of get well wishes and the generous gifts sent during my stay in Minnesota.

Rest assured that my morale is high, I am making an excellent recovery - under the expert care of the Mayo Clinic doctors - and expect to enjoy good health in the very near future.

Once again, thank you for your thoughtfulness in writing and for the gifts which I will always treasure - I also greatly appreciate your prayers and support for the children of the world as well as your genuine concern for my well-being.

Queen Noor joins me in wishing you every possible success on the continuation of your *Walk Around The World*.

I am your sincere friend,

Hussein I

Letter from King Hussein I of Jordan

The International Day of Peace

It was during this time that I met Deborah Moldow at the World Peace Prayer Society and her colleague Monica Willard, both of whom would become dear friends and have supported me for decades. I'd say they planted a seed to always remember children, to put them first. We met a year or so before at the World Peace Festival in Amenia, New York. They invited me to attend the Student Observance for the International Day of Peace at the United Nations. this was the second annual Student Observance organized by the UN Department of Public Information (DPI) for The International Day of Peace (Peace Day). The UN established Peace Day in 1981 and celebrated it on the opening day of the General Assembly. In 2001, a second UN resolution expanded the observation by adding the call for a global day of ceasefires and by setting the annual date of September 21st for the International Day of Peace.

Deborah and Monica worked with the UN DPI to organize the 1998 Student Observance that was held in the Dag Hammarskjold Auditorium. The youth and all those attending the event were invited to the UN plaza for a special celebration. I held the UN flag, leading a quiet parade of children through the back of the UN General Assembly Hall then to the front entrance of the UN Headquarters. At that moment, the children got to see the UN at work. It was a prestigious act, marching with the children through the United Nations, and a *big deal* to have children in the General Assembly. I felt so humbled and honored.

We went on to the front entrance and observed the Minute of Silence for Peace and held a World Peace Flag Ceremony, sending our messages for peace to every UN Member State with the prayer, "May Peace Prevail on Earth!" Earlier, Secretary-General Kofi Annan rang the UN Peace Bell, which the people of Japan donated to the

UN in 1954. It is only rung twice a year—the first day of spring and on every opening day of the yearly UN General Assembly.

What a sight it was, and what a punctation of the message that children are the key to international world peace. Special guests included Mrs. Nane Annan (wife Kofi Annan, Secretary-General of the United Nations) and Mohammad Ali, on the day he became a UN Messenger of Peace.

Because of Deborah and Monica, I have celebrated the International Day of Peace annually, sharing the message of peace from wherever I am around the world.

Monica said, "Thank you for sharing your life to build world peace, one step at a time."

CHAPTER 10:

Marines—Hands Across the Sea

In the fall of 1998, I flew to London and resumed my planning and preparation for the European walk. I was committed to walk for children My focus was on children who could not defend themselves or speak up, especially children caught in the middle of political violence. Children are not responsible for the wars around them, yet they are the victims.

Traveling throughout Europe, I felt at home because I connected with Marine units, both US and European Marines. They were my supporting comrades, the "Hands Across the Sea" (referring to the 1899 marching song of Marine Corps band director John Phillip Sousa). The first stop was the US Embassy in London. Detachment Commander Gunnery Sergeant Mark Lang was in charge. The gunny vetted me and got permission from the

State Department to allow me to stay on the compound. I was treated like a VIP, and the Marines embraced me like family. Off-duty, the Marines and I socialized and watched movies together as I described where and why I was walking. As with my previous walks, the logistics, route, connections, and accommodations were taken care of.

"I receive much more than I give, and it's not just a bed and a meal. It is being accepted for what I'm trying to do," I told a *Stars and Stripes* reporter.

The photograph (taken in front of the US Embassy) and article "Marine's Journey Takes Him Far" reached 3.4 million readers in Europe and Asia. The article also had a picture of Johnny Lu's pearl cross, and I needed it to be held securely in safekeeping until God revealed to me who would receive it. For this task, I trusted the Marines at the US Embassy in London.

Embassy duty for Marines is considered a high-profile, primo assignment. An embassy is a representation of the United States government on foreign soil, and the Marines assigned to protect and defend the embassy and the ambassador at all costs. I witnessed how professional and dedicated these men were. While I was there, the USMC commandant, General Charles C. Krulak, arrived with the sergeant major of the Marine Corps for an inspection of the troops in the Marine barracks of the US Embassy.

As I walked down the steps, the General saw me and said, "Sergeant Garcia, what are you doing in my house?"

"Sir!"

I immediately and instinctively snapped to attention; back straight, head up, and arms pinned to my side. I knew that voice, and General Krulak knew me. I don't think he was surprised (generals are not often caught off-guard), and I was grateful for his acknowledgment. I quietly slipped away while the commandant and the Corps sergeant major continued with the military inspection of the troops.

Later that evening, I was invited to the Marine barracks for a social gathering. General Krulak was happy to see me, and I was honored to cross paths with him once more. I told the general about my plans to walk across Europe and thanked him for the letter he sent me in 1997. From the time I served with him at North Island in 1974 to meeting him at the US Embassy in London in 1998, he rose from the rank of major to four-star general. I was struck by his down-to-earth style and his love and support for each individual Marine, including me. He believed in me and opened the door for Marines all over the world to help me. From this point on, every embassy in Europe welcomed me.

The commandant introduced me to the Corps sergeant major and told him to help me with the walk. He was supportive and agreed to connect me with his best friend, another sergeant major in Scotland. In the interim, though, I traveled to Ireland, where I would present the pearl cross.

Ireland, Land of Green Pastures

The people of Ireland often saw troubled times. When I arrived there, some segments, split along religious lines (Unionist/ Protestant vs. Catholics in Northern Ireland), continued to fight for a unified Ireland, separate from the rule of the British. Northern Ireland and England experienced domestic threats against the collective United Kingdom. I was aware of the conflict as I headed to Dublin, Ireland, and then to the northern city of Omagh, the site of another horrific bombing involving children.

Irish national TV broadcasted an interview with me. The host compared me to Forrest Gump and queried about my route, my motivation, and my shoes.

"I normally walk in areas where prayer and healing are needed. When I get to Omagh, I want to touch as many people as I can." The whole country knew about my walk and that I was coming.

"When will you stop walking?" a reporter asked me.

"I don't know if I will stop, but I do want to thank everyone for being so kind and friendly. I knew I would love the walk in Ireland," I said.

Other guests on the TV program were the president of the Guinness beer company and singer Joan O'Neil, mother of Mel C ("Sporty Spice" of the English band Spice Girls).

Joan said, "From time to time, my husband's group and I are invited to the USA to perform. We enjoy the USA."

We shared stories about Joan's life, her husband's gifted talents as a musician, and their home in Liverpool, England. Talking about the music scene energized me. This connection with Joan later led to an invitation for Joan and her group, Deep River, to perform with Bruce Stephen Foster at the Count Basie Theater in New Jersey. (All were surprised when Sporty Spice made a surprise appearance and performed with her mom!)

While preparing for my walk, a member of the Omagh City Council and Tourist Bureau was charged with organizing my walk. He invited me to stay with him and his family, and they took loving care of me. He enjoyed talking about America, the land of opportunity and, although he had never been to America, he'd heard about Times Square and the tall buildings.

"I am fascinated by how there is so much diversity among people who live in America," he said.

He shared a conversation with me over a brew on his porch as the evening ended. We talked about the beauty of his homeland of Ireland. My new friend expressed how much he loved his wife and children, and I was touched by his sincerity. He was not a Marine, and yet he planned and organized all aspects of my walk in Ireland (Dublin, Omagh, and Belfast). He outlined the route, including places to stay, food, and security.

After hearing about the bombing tragedy in Omagh, I decided the children of Omagh should receive the beautiful pearl cross which Johnny Lu gave me. The cross would be dedicated to the children who died in the bombing.

Scotland Yard on Duty

On the route from Dublin, as I was walking, I noticed a suspicious car that had passed me. Security for my walk included the world-renowned Scotland Yard. Unbeknownst to me, Scotland Yard was observing and watching every move I made to ensure my safety. And thank God!

Suddenly, the car made an abrupt *U*-turn and began driving toward me. Then, from out of nowhere (there must have been brushes and trees along the road), several Scotland Yard agents sprang forth and swiftly encircled the vehicle and its driver. I looked back and saw that the driver had been taken out and spread against the car, and Scotland Yard was interrogating her. I immediately snapped my head straight ahead and *kept walking* as if nothing had happened. My escort driver was a wee bit frightened, though.

The beauty of Ireland is difficult to put into words: deep and lush green grass, and fields with hearty horses, cows, and livestock occasionally swishing their tails. The livestock grazed with such peace and tranquility. And the people were absolutely lovely. After a couple of days of walking, they would wave their hands with excitement and say "Hello!" The road was narrow, and cars had to squeeze by me to get along their way. Some cars were content to follow behind me at my walking pace, enjoying watching me walk in the land of color.

On the northerly route between Dublin and Omagh, there was ongoing fighting and feuds between different groups. I couldn't say for sure who they were or what side they were on. While walking along the road, I could hear gunshots. My route took me right in the direction of the gunfire. Were they shooting at each other? As quickly as I heard the shots, I noticed the gunfire suddenly stopped.

You see, the people heard on TV that I was walking for children and world peace.

"Could it be that God has stopped the shots so that I won't be harmed?" I thought. "Wow, wouldn't that be cool?"

I believe the message of peace encouraged a cease-fire, for a brief time, to consider the possibilities of peace. (This same cease-fire moment also happened in the Philippines; that is another book.)

Shortly thereafter, several men spotted me walking on the road and approached me. What were they thinking? Did they want to shoot me? No, they wanted to shake my hand.

"We heard about you on national television! We wanted to thank you for what you are doing. In fact, we want to invite you for a drink at our pub," the men said.

"Sure! Let's go," I replied.

They swiftly hoisted me upon their shoulders and carried me to a local tavern. At the quaint establishment, everyone laughed and clapped as I was escorted in and surrounded with much merriment and glee. The crowd of about twenty revelers burst into "one of our favorite songs, Oh Danny Boy!"

Oh Danny boy, the pipes, the pipes are calling
From glen to glen, and down the mountainside
The summer's gone, and all the roses falling
'Tis you, 'tis you must go and I must bide
But come ye back when summer's in the meadow
Or when the valley's hushed and white with snow
'Tis I'll be here in sunshine or in shadow
Oh Danny boy, oh Danny boy, I love you so
But come ye back when summer's in the meadow
Or when the valley's hushed and white with snow
'Tis I'll be here in sunshine or in shadow
Oh Danny boy, oh Danny boy, I love you so
Oh Danny boy, oh Danny boy, I love you so
(Lyrics by Frederic Edward Weatherly, 1910)

I was overcome and filled with joy. The deeply emotional lyrics and the conviction of the singers made me weep. I soaked in their love, expressed in traditional song, as tears ran down my face. What a beautiful surprise to feel so welcome and loved by the Irish men, to not feel alone. We drank and sang and sang, and as the celebration continued through the night, I told them about my walk. The Irish appreciated my walk and loved to hear about what I was doing. I don't know what faction may have been entertaining me that night, but I do know that, for one night, they stopped fighting and embraced kindness and good cheer. I was given a cozy room for the night, and the next morning I continued in the peace and the joy of the Lord toward Omagh, not knowing what to expect.

Upon my arrival in Omagh, several people were waiting as I entered the city: the media, members of the District Council, and city folk. Everyone was so happy, which astounded me knowing that city had recently lost twenty-nine people, including children and a pregnant mother, in the bombing. Another two-hundred-twenty were wounded from both sides of the political fight and the religious denominations. The town greeters directed me to the Omagh District Council, and my feet seemed to move in slow motion as the leaders guided me into the building.

As I entered the council chamber, my eyes popped wide open in amazement. To my surprise, the Council seats were not filled with the elected officials, but with children! It would be the children of the city of Omagh who would accept the pearl cross. Everyone was speechless as the graceful children welcomed me and received the pearl cross on behalf of the families of the twenty-five children killed in the Omagh bombing. God gave me words of comfort and compassion for Omagh, and they were touched by the Spirit of God.

"We are so sorry for what happened here in Omagh. I want you to know how much we love you," I explained to the youth who displayed strength, dignity, and resiliency in their sorrow. It was a great time with those kids, and they had so many questions about my walk.

"Do you walk in the rain?"

"You are in so many countries. How do you speak so many languages?"

"What about your sneakers? Who makes them? Can you walk fast in them?"

At that moment, I took off my sneakers, answered their questions, and presented my sneakers, as well, as a gift (and yes, I had another pair waiting).

"Danny, tell everyone you meet that we are grateful for the messages of support and prayer which we received from all over the world, and which have helped to nourish and sustain us emotionally and spiritually through a difficult and traumatic time." This was the message of the Council Chairman, Sean Clarke.

"Continue to spread your message of love and peace, and thank you for thinking of us in this selfless way," he said.

Mr. Clarke said the city of Omagh would put the Pearl Cross in a special place where everyone in Omagh would see it. They loved the cross and the sneakers. The people of Omagh did not want me to leave, but I had to press on to Belfast.

I continued to Belfast, and there the lord mayor of Belfast, city officials, and the media were waiting with a reception. The people were so grateful for the walk for the children, and their support encouraged me to go on, for them. The lord mayor was kind and gracious and said, "You are always welcome."

One day, I would like to go back to Ireland and visit these people of deep conviction and lively spirit. My time in Belfast was extremely short because the airline KLM offered to fly me from Dublin to Glasgow, Scotland. I was driven back to Dublin to board an airline flight.

God had a surprise for me on the KLM flight: an invitation to the cockpit, sitting with the pilot and co-pilot! That was my assigned seat for the flight—what an adventure. I felt like God's kid, traveling on his carpet.

Scotland, The Royal Marines

In Glasgow, Scotland, Sergeant Major Kenny Dalton and his troops of the Royal Marines Reserve met me at the airport and whisked me away to the Royal Marines barracks. My arrival was well-publicized, so they knew I was coming and already had a team assembled and ready to walk. The Royal Marines planned all the stops with a timetable and were ready to clock fifty miles (or eighty kilometers) a day. Based on the route and timeline, the Royal Marines would also notify the media through Headquarters ahead of time. Sgt Major Dalton introduced me to his escort driver, and all were excited.

Sgt Major Dalton was tall and well-built, gung-ho with a can-do attitude. His troops respected him, covered his back, and always did what he told them to do. They were a very disciplined unit, tightly knit. With the Royal Marines, I felt secure with military brethren. Prior to the start of the walk, I briefed everyone about the mechanics of distance walking, especially about being alert and making sure that vehicles wouldn't try to cut in front of the Sgt Major and me, the walkers.

I noticed the Sgt Major was wearing boots.

"Do you have sneakers? The leather boots will cut into your feet after twenty or so miles," I cautiously advised.

"It's OK, I'll be all right," replied Sgt Major Dalton confidently.

I remember when I wore braces on my knees, as one reporter suggested. After the first twenty miles, I ripped off the braces and threw them away. The braces stopped my circulation and were painful. I never did that again. My hands and feet swelled, and I felt like they would explode from lack of circulation.

With the Royal Marines covering logistics, I could walk and talk to God. Most of the time, I did not talk, I just listened. When walking fifty miles a day, it is important that you listen to the Lord and to what your body is saying. We started from George Square in Glasgow on a bright morning, October 2, 1998, with sights set on reaching the US Embassy in London, England—a five-hundred-forty-kilometer (or three-hundred-thirty-five-mile) journey.

For the first three miles, we mentally prepared, settled into a walking groove and steadied our pace. We also had to focus and be observant of our surroundings. Our stride, pace, arm swing, and breathing all came into play. All kinds of questions ran through my mind as the walk unfolded.

"How do the clothes feel, including socks and sneakers?"

"How is the weather and the forecast?"

"What is the terrain, and what obstacles are ahead?"

"Is the escort vehicle too close or too far away?"

"Are there potholes, snakes, wild dogs?"

People who used their cell phones while driving—distracted drivers—were a danger, as were bicyclists who did not pay enough attention to others on the road.

Sgt Major Dalton walked, and walked, and walked with me. He talked, sometimes about his family and his father. We seemed to have a lot in common. Fortunately, the weather was fabulous, and the scenery was amazing. I saw sheep running over the flourishing emerald-green grass. The Royal Marines played the song from *Braveheart*, reminding me of the movie, which I truly enjoyed. When we were not walking, the young Marines shared stories about their countrymen and their lives in the Royal Marines. We talked about our cultures and what we like to eat. The eggs were fresh, and the sourdough bread thick and stretchy. They encouraged me to try a dark sausage, which they loved.

"Danny, this is a common dish. It's eaten for breakfast, lunch, or dinner. We want you to try it. Everyone here eats it. Would you like to try it?"

Not wanting to be rude, I took one bite of the black pudding (a type of pork-blood sausage mixed with grits and barley), and that was it. I couldn't take it, not another bite. Perhaps as peanut butter or the taste of beer is to others, blood pudding is an acquired taste.

"It's not like your New York City pizza, right?" they chuckled.

The Royal Marines teased me, and we all got a great big laugh. We got to know each other as brothers. This interaction was an application of the human relations elements I taught in the US Marine Corps. Such laughter and camaraderie helped the Marines in the escort vehicle to remain focused because following us at five miles an hour for ten hours made for a very long, monotonous day.

For Sgt Major Dalton and me, the pain in our feet, legs, and body grew greater with each passing day. We counted down the miles and the hours until we could stop and rest. One evening, we stopped overnight in a picturesque bed-and-breakfast tavern, and the owner was extraordinary. The owner had a metallic (maybe gold-plated) prosthetic arm with colorful buttons. They called him the "Bionic Man," and all he had to do was speak with his mind and the arm would respond to his command. I was entranced and had never seen anything like it.

"Here are your rooms," he said. "When you are ready, come down, and dinner will be ready for you."

The owner was generous and kind. He treated all of us like royalty. When I entered my charming room, I thought about taking a nice hot bath. So before going downstairs to dinner, I took that hot bath. As I sank into the warm, soothing water, I was overwhelmed once again by the power of love. Tears flowed freely down my face. The water, the Bionic Man, the Royal Marines—God placed His gentle touch on my heart and provided everything according to His plan.

The next day, we continued, and Sgt Major Dalton was really hurting. His leather boots continued to cut into his skin. It was too late to change to sneakers, and he would not quit.

Marines never quit!

Marines don't cry, and that applies to Royal Marines.

As I continued into England, I walked through Birmingham and rested for the weekend. *The Birmingham Evening Mail* (now *Birmingham Mail*) caught up with me for an interview. It was in Brum (short for Birmingham) where the local paper wrote the story "Real Gump Walks into Brum" and printed pictures of both me and Tom Hanks.

"You can't avoid the similarities," I commented to the *Birmingham Evening Mail*, "and I don't mind them at all. I hadn't seen the movie *Forrest Gump* until I went through my own divorce. Like Forrest, when I started walking, I didn't know what I was doing. I would say the movie started it all off. Now the thing has escalated to where I'm walking across the world."

The next stop was Manchester, where food and lodging were graciously provided for me. I had been walking at night to make up time. Potholes in the road were increasingly hazardous for both me and the escort vehicle. I was careful in walking to not twist my ankle. The narrow two-lane roads were also tricky and perilous at night. We devised a makeshift solution and put a string of lights on my body so that drivers could see me and so that I could see where I was walking. It was an odd sight, I suppose. The lights, although clunky, served a purpose: to keep me safe.

For the last few miles of the five-hundred-forty-mile trek from Glasgow to London, the troops asked, "Sgt Major Dalton, do you want to ride in the Humvee?"

He declined.

With a smile, Sgt Major Dalton glanced at me and said, "I will *never* walk with you again."

I parted from the Royal Marines of Scotland and cherish fond memories as well as the highest regard for Sgt Major Kenny Dalton and the Royal Marines Reserve.

In London, England, I received a royal welcome from the commanding officer of the Royal Marines. They accompanied me to the US Embassy, where I reunited with the US Marines. I visited the office of the Prince of Wales and presented my walking stick as a gift, which was received by one of his staff, Henrietta Rolston. His Royal Highness was appreciative of the gift and sent me his congratulations and best wishes for the success of my world trip, to end in Australia at the Olympics in 2000.

ST. JAMES'S PALACE
LONDON SW1A 1BS

From: The Office of HRH The Prince of Wales

5th November, 1998

Dear Mr. Garcia,

The Prince of Wales has asked me to thank you for your gift presented to him whilst on your walk for the Children of England and for peace.

His Royal Highness appreciates your kindness in giving him the walking stick. It was most generous of you and The Prince of Wales has asked me to send you his congratulations and best wishes for the success of your World trip ending in Australia at the Olympics in the year 2000.

Yours sincerely,

Miss Henrietta Rolston

Thank you from the Prince of Wales

Netherlands, The Dutch Marines

Crossing the North Sea by air, I landed in the Netherlands for the next leg of my European walk. This time, the Korps Mariniers, Dutch Marines of the Netherlands, joined me. I started on the North Sea coastline at the Hague, or Den Haage in Dutch, the seat of power of the Netherlands. The Hague is well-guarded, and I had the opportunity to visit the historical site.

Not to be outmatched or outmarched by an American, the Dutch sent me a ringer in Sgt Major Ben Schouten. He was a tall mariner, and for every step Ben took, I had to take three steps to keep up with him. The Dutch Marines chose him as my walking companion because he could walk fast and for long distances.

As we traveled through Rotterdam, the challenges of terrain and weather confronted us. Treacherous rains and strong winds hit us on day one. We were crossing a narrow bridge, and the gusts were so powerful that they were literally blowing us off the bridge.

I squinted through the rain and saw that the wind was forcing Sgt Major Schouten over the railing. He had a high center of gravity, being tall and slender. The men in the Humvees wanted to come out and give aid, but that would have put all of us in peril.

"Take my hand! You have to reach out and take my hand!" I shouted at my lanky walking mate and clung to my side of the bridge. I could not reach him if I held on to the railing, and he could not reach me if he continued to clutch his side of the bridge railing. There was only one way: we would both have to let go to meet in the middle so I could grab him. In the turbulent gale, we had to trust God and trust each other.

"One, two, three . . . *now!*"

We both let go of the bridge and lunged toward each other. I seized the sergeant major, pulled him toward my side of the bridge, and grasped him and the bridge tightly. Together, battling the power of the rain and gusts, we painstakingly crossed the bridge. We took one slow step at a time, straining together, relying on our combined fortitude. We reached the end of the bridge and jumped into the Humvees safely. I was reminded of Jesus with his disciples in the storm, how he encouraged them and calmed their fears.

We proceeded through Holland and hiked through the mush of fields where we saw water dikes nestled throughout. It was cold and muddy sloshing through the lowlands in late October of 1998. I appeared on a Dutch television show, *Breakfast TV*, being interviewed in the military camp in Rotterdam. It was both a great challenge and a great walk.

I crossed into Belgium and arrived in Brussels, considered to be the capital of Belgium and the de facto capital of the European Union. I stayed at the US Embassy with the Marines and made friends quickly. I also spent a few nights in the Christian Center de Rhode-Saint-Genèse. The center had many kids who encircled me and showered me with hugs and love. I couldn't speak Dutch or French, and they couldn't speak English or Spanish, yet they knew I loved them and that I was walking for them. The children did not want me to leave. The children loved me back. Journalist Janine Claeys interviewed me for the paper *Le Soir* (Nov 12, 1998). I told her about my mission from God, walking and praying for children and peace, and about the brotherhood amongst fellow Marines.

Paris, US Marine Corps Ball

From Brussels, I went southwest to Paris, France. The weather was chilly, and there was a great deal of snow on the ground. Fortunately, the Marines I had left in Belgium treated me to a shopping spree of cold-weather boots and clothing. I was expecting a

Red Cross vehicle, which did not show up, so I started marching alone in the snow.

The snow was up to my knees, and with a fifty-pound pack on my back, every step was difficult. I remember falling face-first in the snow, exhausted and feeling isolated in the serene, white landscape.

"Get up, keep going, don't quit!" the silent voice within me said.

I struggled to my feet, regained my breath, and decided to detour to find a café and a hot cup of coffee. Then I looked up at the horizon and saw a big red cross. The French Red Cross truck had found me! I was so thankful.

It was about 9:00 p.m. one evening when I arrived at the US Embassy in Paris. The Marines were waiting for me. While there, I was able to see the beauty of Paris. The embassy itself was always so busy. People came in and out all the time.

A big celebration was coming up. Some of the men asked me, "Do you know that the Marine Corps Ball is right around the corner? Are you ready to attend the ball? It will be in a fancy hotel. Can you join us?"

The Marine Corps' birthday is November 10th. Marines all over the world attend a ball, usually on a weekend, and wear their formal dress blues for the occasion. The ball was being held that following weekend.

"I'm sorry, but I've been walking through the snow. I don't have any clothes for the gala."

"Oh, don't worry, we already took care of that. Tomorrow morning you have an appointment with our tux guy," said the Marines. "He's going to take care of what you need."

Remember Cinderella? At that moment, I think I know what she felt like. Then, when I saw the place where the ball was being held, well, I really knew I was in for a treat. The venue was opulent. We had a beautiful table with champagne and all the trimmings. Dignitaries and generals from different countries attended. It was an incredible evening.

Like Cinderella, I was transformed in a few blinks from carrying a fifty-pound pack with all my belongings, walking through a snowstorm, to being finely dressed as a gentleman attending the Marine Corps Ball. It was like two different worlds, and the Marines had gone all-out to take care of me.

Switzerland and a UN Conference

Next stop: Geneva, Switzerland. Geneva is located on the southern tip of Lake Geneva, and the border of France is a few kilometers away. This is where the United Nations Office at Geneva (UNOG) is located. In Geneva, I stayed in the US Embassy with my USMC brothers. It was a beautiful day in Switzerland, and the city and people were so beautiful and friendly.

Somehow (and by whom I do not recall), I was invited to and attended a UN conference. The attendees were well-dressed. Everyone seemed important and to be a dignitary of some kind. I, on the other hand, was dressed in my walking attire. As I entered the conference room, I was assigned a seat in the front. I did not know the theme of the conference, the topic to be discussed, or any of the participants. As I listened to the conferees talk about differences and problems, I felt very uncomfortable. In my spirit, I felt I had to change the direction of the conversation.

I raised my right hand politely and held it up. I waited to be recognized and to be given an opportunity to speak. My thoughts raced. What am I going to say to change their perspectives, their communications? What could I, of all people, offer to solve the problems at hand?

I did not know what I was going to say, but I seized the moment.

The moderator asked me, "Mr. Garcia, you have been walking around the world. What would you like to say?"

With the prompting of the Holy Spirit of God, I stood up with confidence and stated boldly, distinctly, and loudly, "*I am not a minority.*"

The words left my lips and shocked me. These five words hushed the group and sunk into the collective consciousness of the moment, elevating their focus and thoughts. I had their attention. Then the conferees stood up and gave me a standing ovation. After the conference, a young gentleman approached me.

"Mr. Garcia, Diane Watson, the US ambassador to Micronesia, would like to speak to you," he said.

Had I embarrassed the ambassador? I did not know what to expect. Ambassador Watson introduced herself and, to my surprise, congratulated me on what I said. She extended an invitation for me to visit Micronesia and stay in the embassy.

"The waters around Micronesia are astounding," said Ambassador Watson. "You can see underwater sea life and sunken vessels from the past. Whenever you have some time off from your walk, please come. We would love to have you. Maybe we can even organize a walk for children and world peace in Micronesia." What an honor!

International School of Geneva

After the UN conference, I explored Geneva, an international crossroads. I had the opportunity to reach children of many nationalities. It was December 9, 1998. I met with the principal and teachers at the International School of Geneva—a unique atmosphere, and the first international school in the world. Children from all over the world attended this school. The three thousand students represented one-hundred-fifteen nationalities and spoke eighty-five languages. I described my walk to the administrators and told them I would like to share my adventure with the international students.

Thrilled, the principal called for a special student assembly with me as the guest speaker. The students were arrayed in a semicircle, sitting on benches and eager to hear my first words. As I began to speak, the assembly was quiet enough to hear a pin drop. I thanked the school for allowing me to share my experiences, especially the treacherous ones.

"Yes, in the United States I walked over a rattlesnake and turned around to see its tail rattling and its long tongue flickering at me. I was almost struck by lightning. I've had to rebuke a pack of wild dogs that were going to attack me."

The real stories captured the students' awe and interest, and they wanted to hear more. The students, hearts pounding rapidly, had their eyes glued upon me as they waited for my next words. I noticed that children in all parts of the world have similar questions and that they also have deep pain, even in such a prestigious environment. So, I paused and knew it was time to share a simple message from the heart.

"I want you to know that I love you. Yes, I love each one of you. You are special in God's eyes and He told me to tell you. Every step I take is for you because of His love for you. Even though it is dangerous sometimes, and I sometimes I feel like my body is going to break from the pain, I won't quit. With God's help, I can't stop. Everyone needs to know how important you are to Him. No matter what you are going through, don't quit."

The aura of God settled on the children and opened their eyes and hearts to understand the reason why I walk. The message of love penetrated their young hearts. God was calling out to them, drawing them closer to Him on that day.

Suddenly, two teenage girls burst from the stands and came racing toward me. The onlooking students were shocked, frozen in amazement and anticipation of what would happen next.

"What is Mr. Garcia going to do?" they must have thought. I remembered how Jesus welcomed children.

I held my breath. I did not know what was happening. The two girls ran up to me, and I instinctively stretched out my arms widely to receive them. They dashed into my embrace and flung their arms around me tightly. The girls buried their precious faces into me. I was shocked and surprised by their spontaneous display of affection. They squeezed me so tightly that I could not break free or let them go.

I tilted and lowered my head to one side to hear one of the girls whispering:

"Danny, today we were going to commit suicide after school," she confided. "After so many years, our parents told us we were really not their children. We found out today that our parents are not our parents and that we are adopted. We needed to know. They did not tell us the truth. We felt they really did not love us, so we planned it out and made a pact to kill ourselves."

The girls, devastated and feeling betrayed, said they wanted to die.

They continued through sobs, "Then you came, saying you *loved us*, and we now have hope. We don't want to commit suicide now."

Imagine, the words of God's love, spoken sincerely and with conviction. It is God's love that surpasses all circumstances and cuts through the darkness. God's love is strong enough to erase suicidal thoughts. I know this because I was suicidal more than once and wanted to kill myself and die before the love of Jesus saved me.

I wonder when was the last time the girls were told they were loved. God knew they needed to hear the message, and I was His vessel that day. I experienced a curious mix of relief and astonishment at the same time.

To know that God would use me to save lives was humbling. This experience with the girls at the school was a confirmation that my walk and my demonstration of love *did matter*. My walks made a difference for life or death.

This is heavy—profound even. This was God's amazing grace.

Hungary and Italy

News of my walk had spread to Hungary, and Action News TV flew me from Geneva to Budapest, Hungary, to appear on a special Christmas program. I remember it being snowy and the plane landing on the snow-packed runway. A limousine was waiting for me, and the chauffeurs took me to a hotel. Action News sponsored my airfare and provided food and lodging. The limo service took me wherever I wanted to go. I was featured on the TV news magazine *Frei-Dasszie* viewed by millions in Hungary and in sixteen European countries. During that same TV program lineup, who else but Tom Hanks was being interviewed before me! I missed him, though, and did not personally meet him then.

The reporter was Tamas Frei. He won the Hungarian Joseph Pulitzer Prize twice, traveled worldwide as a war correspondent, and was one of Hungary's most respected television reporters. Action News had heard that I was going to Rome to visit Pope John Paul II (again). They wanted to be part of it by broadcasting from the Vatican a Christmas greeting to the Hungarian people on Christmas Eve. The Hungarians arranged a walk with me and some children. In the snow, hundreds of young Boy Scouts and Pioneers walked with me from Budapest to the news studio, promoting world peace and the Christmas spirit. Any time spent with children was a great time. I also stopped at the US Embassy, toured the facility, and met with the Marines. They were collecting toys for the Toys for Tots program.

Action News helped me to travel to Rome, where I presented (in December 1998) my walking stick and a song to His Holiness Pope John Paul II. I thought the pope would appreciate the song, so I presented it to him. I was honored to receive a letter of gratitude from the Vatican secretariat of state, in which Pope John Paul II imparted to me his Apostolic blessing!

SECRETARIAT OF STATE

From the Vatican, January 26, 1999

Dear Mr. Garcia,

The Holy Father wishes me to express his gratitude for the walking-stick and song which you presented to him. He very much appreciates your devoted sentiments.

His Holiness asks our Lord Jesus Christ to sustain you in his grace and love as you continue your walk for children's rights and peace in the world. He cordially imparts to you his Apostolic Blessing.

Sincerely yours,

Monsignor Pedro López Quintana
Assessor

Pope John Paul imparts his Apostolic Blessing to Danny Garcia

The song presented to the pope had special significance to my mission of walking for children and world peace. Earlier in 1998, Bruce Stephen Foster created the song, titled "Children of Our World," as a theme song for my walk around the world for children.

The following chapter describes my dear friendship and collaboration spanning decades with Bruce Stephen Foster. It is a tale of song-writing inspiration and friendship.

CHAPTER 11:

Cousin Bruce, Music Man

Music has been so important in my life since my early days in Spanish Harlem with my father, to during Woodstock, and throughout my concert-producing days. It has brought me joy and helped me to heal. I have never been far from music and look for ways to incorporate music in my walks. I have had help from my beloved friend—the talented yet humble Grammy Award nominee, musician, and artist—Bruce Stephen Foster. He is quite the storyteller and has over 1,000 songs committed to memory. We've done concerts together on three continents, produced a CD, and shared our lives as brothers.

My first memory of Bruce was hearing a song he wrote and sang on TV for Frank Sinatra. Bruce's commemoration of Frank Sinatra in an original song moved me, and I decided to contact him. That call was the beginning of an enduring and fruitful friendship.

I'd like Bruce to tell you the story about our bond of music and brotherhood, in his words.

The Children of Our World

My adventures with Danny Garcia began out of the blue in the spring of 1998. A series of coincidences and probable divine guidance led Danny to my musical "front door." He had recently seen me singing on Fox News in a broadcast from Hoboken, New Jersey.

It was Frank Sinatra's eightieth birthday, and I was performing a song live on the air that I had written with a Hoboken native named Ed Shirak. It was Shirak who founded the Frank Sinatra Museum in a building next door to where Sinatra was born.

The song, titled "A Time That Was," was an anthem to Mr. Sinatra and somewhat of a love letter to Sinatra from the people of Hoboken. This was the evening news show that Sinatra watched every night from his home in California.

I consider it to be one of the great honors of my life to have looked into the news camera after I finished the song and said, "Happy birthday, Mr. Sinatra," knowing Frank was watching at that very moment.

Danny Garcia was also watching that show and was touched by the song and jotted down my name. Danny was just embarking on a walk across America for children's rights.

When he reached New Jersey, Danny called me and asked me if I would write an inspirational song that would accompany his ongoing mission to help children everywhere.

We set up a meeting, and I was immediately impressed with his fervor and sincerity. At the meeting's end, I knew what I needed to write, so I threw the guitar in the back seat of my classic 1975 AMC Pacer and drove over to Sandy Hook Beach for inspiration.

I found a spot where my front tires were actually in the sand with a close-up view of the ocean. I began writing with the ocean in front of me. A thunderstorm that looked like it was directed by Steven Spielberg was raging.

A storm was approaching, and huge waves were crashing on the beach in front of me. Low, black clouds were bubbling and swirling overhead. There were lightning strikes hitting the beach a hundred yards away. This was more inspiration than I could have hoped for!

The song "The Children of Our World" was born as a force of nature and baptized by fire. My beloved old Pacer and I never shared a more profound moment.

I had released my second solo album in America called *Reality Game*, and "The Children of Our World" was on it. Danny took my song and presented it to Pope John Paul II, who blessed it. I'd like to think of it as a sign that the song has a certain destiny to benefit the children of our world.

One of my early memories of being part of the ongoing adventures of Danny Garcia was in February 1999. Danny had just gotten back from a prayer walk in the Middle East. I retrieved him from JFK Airport, and we headed into New York for a meeting with a prominent New York City businessman who was intrigued by Danny's dedication and fervor. His name was Johnny Lu of LuCoral, one of the largest pearl farmers in the world.

It was a blustery day, with the temperature in the mid-twenties. We were slogging through an inch or two of slushy snow, and Danny had on only the sweatshirt he wore on the plane. No hat or gloves. I offered to stop at the first place where we could get him gloves and warmer clothes.

Without further thought, Danny replied, "No need for that. God will take care of me."

I replied with a subtle shrug.

As we continued to scurry to our appointment a few blocks away, Danny sees something in the street.

"Hey Bruce, look at that!" And there, in the street, was a pair of men's fur-lined gloves. Although a taxi had run over them, the pair was somehow not yet wet. He picked them up and smiled with delight.

"Perfect fit!" Then he said softly and respectfully, "Thanks, God."

That was the first time it struck me how many little miracles I had already witnessed. Well, there were a lot more to come. Within a few minutes, we were walking into the towering office building, almost late for our meeting. Both elevators were just closing their doors as we kicked the snow off our shoes on the large rubber mat on the lobby floor. As we waited and waited for the elevators to return, Danny was thinking out loud in his usual, inspired fashion.

"I want to do a prayer walk through India."

Danny would need lodging and support wherever he could find it. Since he did everything in his travels through sponsorship from benevolent people who understood his mission, he had to constantly improvise to reach each goal.

He said, "Maybe the Red Cross could help me with food and shelter as I walk through India." He paused to ruminate on his own words . . . then the light in his brain lit up.

"That's it! I have to speak to someone who is part of the Indian chapter of the Red Cross."

The elevator *still* had not reached the ground level, and I expressed my impatience with it. Danny calmly replied, "Everything happens for a reason. Trust that you are being guided, and if we're a few minutes late, that's okay."

The elevator finally came, and we filed in with the crowd. Then, just as the door was almost closed, we heard a voice shouting in a thick Indian accent saying:

"Hold the door, please!"

Yep, it was an Indian guy wearing a Red Cross jacket who ran in from the street and hopped in the elevator with us. I was flabbergasted and speechless. Part of me wondered, "Is this an elaborate setup?"

Danny just looks at me and says, "There you go."

He talked to the gentlemen and immediately got a card from the guy who, as we found out later, turned out to be exactly who Danny wanted to see—the liaison with the Red Cross in India.

One Night of Peace

Shortly before I met Danny, I was on a flight from Newark to Los Angeles to do some songwriting with my former bandmate and cherished friend, Richie Sambora.

Midway over America, my brain downloaded a song and a vision.

A melody and the words "one night of peace" came simultaneously, along with a vision of an event that would invite every nation on earth to have a twenty-four-hour cease fire. I imagined every child on earth having the chance to sleep peacefully through just one night in human history.

I imagined how it might inspire the next generation to grow up to be hopeful instead of hopeless. I imagined if it could be done for twenty-four hours, why not forty-eight hours, why not forever?

When I touched down in LAX, I was on fire. I reached Richie's house and shared the song and the vision with him. His daughter, Ava, was just two years old, and I felt that he was looking at the world with new eyes. Indeed, he was.

We spent the next two days writing the song. We both felt like we had a gift for the world.

Enter Danny Garcia, the person who would carry the message and the song around the world for the next twenty years . . . and counting. Danny loved this song, so he wanted to have a concert. The song and event were to give hope and inspiration to future generations to never give up on *trying* to develop a world culture of peaceful coexistence.

We picked the Count Basie Theater in Red Bank, New Jersey, as the venue. The date was April 3, 1999. We sold out three shows.

We remain forever indebted to all the artists that rallied to perform that night, especially Tim McLoone and Holiday Express, Bobby Bandiera, Dolores and Layonne Holms, Joe Bonnano and the Godsons of Soul, Lee Mrowicki, Mary McNally, Rania Kurdi (a major star in Jordan who flew in for the concert), Sporty Spice (who flew in from England), and many others.

Most importantly, I thank Danny Garcia, a former Marine who put it all together with me. The Count Basie show was the seed.

Later that year, in August of 1999, Danny and I were invited to the fiftieth anniversary of the Geneva Peace Conference. I performed "One Night of Peace" at Geneva's Victoria Hall as part of Fete de' Excellence (Celebration of Excellence). I was the first, and maybe still the only, rock artist invited to perform at the classical venue. Ray Charles played there a few times.

In September of 2000, Danny invited me to perform "One Night of Peace" in Australia. I did an ONOP telecast from Australia at the Hard Rock Café in Sydney that was simulcast to all their venues around the world on the eve of the opening of the Olympic Games. The song was a plea for every nation to honor a twenty-four-hour ceasefire prior to the lighting of the Olympic torch.

I would like to think that I inspired Danny to produce a day-long concert promoting the UN's International Day of Peace. On his back, Danny has carried the words of "One Night of Peace" through North America, Africa, South America, and Europe.

Bruce Stephen Foster, Grammy Nominee
Receives Award for *One Night of Peace*

Danny said, "Bruce's music inspired me in 1998 and still inspires me to this day. That is why I have carried the song 'One Night of Peace' with me through my travels across the globe."

I believe in the power of music and positive thought. I hope to have more adventures with Danny Garcia on his ongoing quest for the children of our world.

CHAPTER 12:

Walking for Children Around the World

After Christmas in Rome in 1998, I was drawn to the Middle East. The Lord told me to go.

It was where the action was. I would walk for the children there. I had a message of peace and the need to protect children everywhere.

Real progress in the Middle East seemed to be in the making between Israel's prime minister Netanyahu and the Palestine Liberation Organization's (PLO) president, Yasir Arafat. But peace in the Middle East has also been elusive, and the tension and disagreements centuries old. Nonetheless, I returned to Israel, asking the Lord to plan my every step. I returned to Jerusalem, the Holy City.

I met with the mayor of Jerusalem, Ehud Olmert, on January 11, 1999. I presented to the mayor my walking stick before my scheduled walk in Israel for children and world peace. He gave me his written blessings with wishes for success in a letter dated January 11, 1999.

"Please be careful, Danny," the mayor warned. The mayor knew I would be traveling into Palestine soon. Who was I? I was a man with a vision of peace, and from my vantage point at that time, sending a message of peace seemed feasible.

לשכת ראש העיר
Mayor's Office
ديوان رئيس البلدية

עיריית ירושלים
Municipality of Jerusalem
بلدية أورشليم – القدس

יובל החמישים לישראל
ISRAEL 50 JUBILEE
٥٠ سنة لدولة اسرائيل

Jerusalem, January 11, 1999
23 Tevet, 5759

Mr. Danny Garcia
Children of Our World Foundation
San Diego, CA
USA

Dear Mr. Garcia,

It was a pleasure to meet with you earlier today. I would like to take this opportunity to congratulate you and your efforts to spread your unique message of peace and the need to protect and support the rights of children around the world.

In this upcoming year, as we near the beginning of the new millenium, let us hope and pray for the peace of our children and people.

With blessings from the City of Peace, Jerusalem I wish you much success in your journey

Sincerely, *Best Wishes*

Ehud Olmert

מינר ספרא 1, ת.ד. 775, ירושלים, 91007, טלפון 6297997-02, פקס 6296014-02

1 Safra Square, POB 775, Jerusalem, 91007, Israel. Tel. 02-6297997 Fax. 02-6296014

ميدان سفرا ١، ص.ب. ٧٧٥، أورشليم – القدس، ٩١، هاتف ٦٢٩٧٩٩٧-٢، فاكس ٦٢٩٦، ١٤-٢.

Letter from Mayor of Jerusalem

Energy and Elevation in the Holy Land

The Holy Land was a place that excited me and elevated me to a higher level of understanding God. In Israel, it is said that the Bible comes alive, and there I received confirmation of what I had read and learned. Being there broadened my vision, and I had high hopes and expectations of new life and new learning. I saw, felt, and appreciated what had been written of the great men who followed and served God.

January 18–21, 1999. The walk in Israel was a continuation of my worldwide walk and took me from Jerusalem to Bethlehem, Haifa to Netanya and Tel Aviv. I decided to walk on behalf of Ilan: the Israel Foundation for Handicapped Children. This organization supported all handicapped children living in Israel and in Palestine.

I started at the Jaffa gate in Jerusalem and walked along the towering walls of the Old City. I felt like I was going back in time. The Old City, as the name implies, is ancient and full of history. I walked in the places where Jesus walked. Walking the cobblestones of the uphill Villa De La Rosa was a dramatic introduction into the Holy City. I felt small and insignificant, as one walking into a mighty kingdom.

The sweltering heat was overwhelming. People, animals, and vehicles bustled around all at the same time. There was so much energy and life in the city.

"When would I get to the top?" I thought.

I stopped and reflected on Jerusalem, like an emerald city leading to the gates of heaven. Jerusalem is unlike any other city or any other country. I felt the reign of God and His sovereignty in the city of Jerusalem.

Throughout Israel, I interacted with people of many different races and religions. I participated in the activities of the marketplaces, highways, and byways. It reminded me of Spanish Harlem in New York, where I grew up, and how everyone, regardless of race, color, or ethnicity got along with respect. The food was colorful, flavorful, and spicy. We talked about my previous walks, and my hosts were curious and attentive to my travels and experiences in other countries.

We celebrated! We laughed!

I rose every day with great expectation to visit the next site, to places where Arabs and Jews coexisted peacefully in trade, in schooling, in worship, and in respect of each other. I was not subjected to violence. I did not experience the turmoil sometimes portrayed in the media. I'm not saying that violence does not exist, only that during this walk I did not witness it.

In fact, it was just the opposite. I saw harmony for the sake of the children. The Israel Foundation for Handicapped Children organization treated both Palestinian and Jewish children equally, and with such care.

What stood out to me was their need and desire to be respected. I kept my ideas and opinions (religious, economic, political, or otherwise) to myself. I treated them with respect, and the people welcomed me. I put myself in their shoes and strove to understand how they live, without changing them. Once again, I applied my human relations background of how to interact with others and how to respect them.

The staff of the foundation supported me and walked with me, climbing hills even in some of the challenging areas in Haifa, which had steep grades. Haifa is a port city, and from the top of the soaring hills, I looked over the sprawling harbor and ships of all kinds in an expansive panoramic display. I was so high in elevation that it seemed I could raise my hands and touch the sky.

Tel Aviv is a major metropolitan and tourist area with shopping, souvenirs, beaches, water activities, and nightlife. Tel Aviv reminded me of San Diego, California. In Tel Aviv, I talked with the Israeli soldiers, both men and women, and asked about their service.

"What is it like to be in the army?"

"How long have you been in? How many years are you in for?"

"What is your training like?"

They were open to listening to me and yet guarded, reserved, and keenly observant. The soldiers were alert to their surroundings and vigilant about their job of security and protection. They were placed in strategic locations where there were large groups of people. As a former Marine and law-enforcement officer with my own extensive security training, I felt safe. The soldiers were well-trained to know how to deal with various situations which could explode at any moment.

I was thankful for my time with the Israeli soldiers and knew it was time to keep moving.

The Hashemite Kingdom of Jordan

Jordan was close by and was my next stop. Jordan had control of the West Bank and, with the help of King Hussein I, was regarded as a more neutral country in the Middle East. My journey in the Hashemite Kingdom of Jordan began in Amman. The Ministry of Youth wrote a letter of support, and then the country opened up for me. In Jordan, I stayed at the US Embassy and began getting things organized to do a walk for King Abdullah II, who had ascended to the throne in 1999, and for his wife, Queen Rania (who is Palestinian).

The queen championed causes for the kingdom and led a "stop smoking" campaign and run. I was invited to participate in the run, from Amman to the Dead Sea, a fifty-mile route. I was the only American. Everyone else ran, but I completed the trail walking. In the heat, I became sick and threw up. Thankfully, I recovered before the grand gala and reception. That's when I met Queen Rania and was one of the few who received a commemorative watch from the queen.

The king encouraged foreign investment to make Jordan more competitive globally. Jordan's only port is the Port of Aqaba at the northernmost point of the Red Sea between the Asian and African continents. The port has always been a strategic logistics point, and King Abdullah II initiated a plan to transform it into a free port, or special economic zone.

To increase publicity for Port Aqaba, I proposed a walk.

The walk from Aqaba north to Amman, the capital, was roughly three-hundred-twenty kilometers (about two hundred miles). The Jordanian Ministry of Tourism and the Jordanian Police sponsored my walk. Before the walk started, a cab driver in Amman stopped me and told me about his son who was eight years old. The boy was a good-looking young man, but his eyes were severely crossed. If not corrected, he would go blind. They needed funds for the eye operation. I included the father's request for his son in my walk from Aqaba to Amman.

So I started walking from Aqaba, where I stopped at the Rosary Sisters School and met with the children there.

While I was walking northward, a major radio station caught wind of the walk and the story of the boy who needed an eye operation. They publicized his need and people generously responded. When I completed the walk in Amman, the cab driver found me.

"Danny, while you were walking, my son had his operation! People heard about my son on the radio and gave us the money we needed."

The young boy's eyes were corrected. He had a successful operation. The father was so elated.

"I want to have a big dinner for you, Danny!"

The cab driver threw a huge party for me to say thank you. We sat on pillows on the floor in front of a large table filled with food and traditional entrées that we ate with our hands. He was not a rich man, but he overflowed with gratitude for what God had done through me for his son.

In September of 1999, I was invited back home to New York City. The United Nations held a Jubillenium Breakfast Launch. That's when I started promoting and presenting interfaith candles as gifts. When I came back to Jordan, the minister of youth wanted me to meet the dowager Queen Noor (widow of the late King Hussein I). I was promoting the Jubillenium initiative and presented her a Jubillenium candle on Earth Day of 2000.

Queen Noor of Jordan (2000)

Jordan to Bagdad with Iraqi Olympians

Amman, due to its central location, had become my staging point to other parts of the Middle East. While I was staying at the US Embassy with the Marines, I had heard about an American congressman urging the lift of the embargo on Iraq so that women could get blood. I thought about the women and their babies. I had heard about how their children were suffering.

"I want to walk for the children of Iraq. I want to walk from Jordan to Iraq," I declared.

The Marines told me, "Danny, we can inform the authorities so you can get permission. We don't know how long it will take, but we will let you know ASAP."

International relations between the US and Iraq were dicey during this time. Saddam Hussein was still in power in Iraq. There were stories of torture during his regime. The US had placed an embargo on Iraq because of its invasion of neighboring Kuwait, and the embargo impacted Iraq economically. Yet, as for myself, I asked, "What about the children?" They have no say in politics and war. The children were victims too.

My government couldn't prohibit me from walking, but could they support it? I did not get involved in politics and international relations, yet I found myself in the middle of international dilemmas.

While I was waiting, I went to the Iraqi consulate and asked for permission to do the walk. They looked at me in shock. They did not speak, but I imagined what they were thinking.

"Who is this American? He wants to walk in our country? Is he mad?"

"I need your help to make this happen," I told them. "It is for the children."

Several times I went to their offices. I was persistent, but not pushy. I did not know what was happening behind the scenes. They were trying to get someone of influence to sponsor and pay for the walk.

Finally, the Iraqi consulate gave me permission. The consulate advised, "Saddam Hussein has a relative who is the president of the Iraqi Olympic Committee. They will sponsor your entire trip."

"We will tell you where to be and direct your steps to the border of Iraq," said the consulate representatives.

When I went back to the US Embassy and told them what happened at the Iraqi consulate, they said, "We haven't heard anything yet."

What could I do? Wait for permission or move ahead?

"Thank you for your help. I really can't wait any longer," I told the US Embassy. "I'm going to take advantage of their hospitality. This walk, like all my walks, will be a prayer walk for the children and peace for Iraq."

"Well," they advised, "if you do go, don't let them stamp your passport."

From Amman, Jordan, to Iraq, I set out on May 6, 2000.

Immediately, I met the Jordanian police, who provided police escort while I walked from Amman to the border of Iraq. At the border, I was met by an Iraqi delegation, reception, media, and some officials from the Iraqi Olympic team.

"Here's where we start the walk on the Iraqi side," said one of the delegates. We had a brief meeting about the walk, which would begin the next morning. They provided a meal and a place to sleep. I had more questions but decided to just be patient and let the walk unfold.

In the morning, I met with the caravan that would be part of the walk. It was an expanded escort with a school bus, bus driver, chef and staff, two military vehicles with mounted auto-matic weapons, a medical team, and five Iraqi Olympic athletes. They also provided a large open-bed truck that had TV cameras mounted and several people filming. My safety was of paramount importance to the Iraqis. Into Baghdad, we took Highway 1, a notoriously dangerous road.

I walked, and the Olympians ran, each rotating their runs during the trek. Our goal was fifty miles a day. Desert tempera-tures were one-hundred-twenty-five degrees in the daytime. The path was all desert, desolate. We took one step at time, averaging eight-to-ten hours a day on Highway 1.

One day, we were hit by a sandstorm, or what is known as a haboob in the Middle East. We had little warning as the dust cloud quickly flew over a dune and engulfed us. Strong and high-speed wind gusts lifted top layers of sand and tossed the sand in every direction and into every crevice.

I coughed, tried to close my eyes, and became disoriented. I had sand in my mouth, in my eyes, and in my ears. I felt like I was suffocating in sand. It was so bad that my companions draped their shawls above me to shield me from the sand and wind. It did not end right away, so we found a place to stay for the night until the storm ceased. I was so grateful to my teammates. They really protected me and kept me safe.

Who Is My Neighbor?

There were times when we saw villages along the highway, but they were few. In one small city, the caravan leader took me and ushered me into a spacious room in what seemed to be a palace. The room had a beautiful red carpet with intricate gold designs. This was a place of greatness, a place of prominence.

Sitting around the room were five hundred elders in traditional Arab dress. Each of them represented their tribe, and they were waiting to hear me speak to them. I was in total awe and in amazement. I was in another world, and I loved it.

In the Muslim culture, guests are to be respected and welcomed, especially when they are strangers or have no family or friends in that country. Muslims are expected to pay attention to their guests, sit with them, and make them feel comfortable.

There is a spiritual element too. For followers of Islam, honoring the guest is tied to the faith of a true believer. Across the world, you will find Muslims doing their best to offer hospitality to the guest in their home or their community. Entertaining a guest is important. It signifies the respect and concern of a host toward his guest and toward God. Hospitality in Islam is a triangle that links God, the guest, and the host.

"As-Salaam-Alaikum," I said. This means "peace be upon you" in Arabic.

"Wa-Alaikum-Salaam" they responded, which means "and unto you, peace."

"I want you to know that I love you," I said to them.

I paused and was intentional with each word I said. I was speaking in English, and they understood me. I had their complete attention, and they listened intently. I told them that I have been walking for children all over the world, including the children of Iraq. My words were simple but powerful and profound.

"I have come so far to do this walk just for you. I am not looking for anything from you. I am here to give you the love that God has given me to give to you freely."

The elders were touched, so much so that they bestowed additional honor and respect beyond welcoming me as a guest in their country. When I stood in front of them, the leaders summoned several people who had garments in their hands. They dressed me and draped me in elegant white, silky garments that covered me completely. They asked me to remove my walking shoes, then they knelt and put my feet into exquisite light-brown leather sandals.

In the beautiful white, flowing garments, I felt and looked like a prince, a sheik, like Lawrence of Arabia. All the elders stood up. I lifted my arms and gracefully twirled the flowing sleeves of my garment, smiling at all of them. They laughed and clapped, and I clapped with them. They gave me an Arab name for "family." At that moment, I felt that the elders had accepted me and that *we were one family.* They treated me like a king, and I felt like I belonged to them.

This episode and memory with the Iraqi elders were personal. My time with them was intimate and genuine. I reached the hearts of people and won their hearts through the love of God. Jesus prepared me and called me to love the world, to love my neighbor.

"You Don't Have Enough Bullets"

As we left the Arab village and continued toward Baghdad, the security patrol noticed something odd. In the distance, the guards saw large groups of people coming toward the caravan. About 20,000 people were walking toward us and were converging on us. The people were coming from both sides of the road. The military escort responsible for my safety became agitated and concerned. The crowds were not racing angrily toward us, but we were clearly outnumbered. Although the vehicles had automatic machine guns at the front and back of the caravan, I think the escorts were afraid.

"What shall we do, Mr. Garcia? They are coming!" the guards exclaimed.

"You don't have enough bullets. Let them come," I said.

As the crowd got closer, I could hear them singing. The caravan came to a stop. The guards were shocked. The people were in unison, in harmony, like a massive choir. The melody was beautiful.

"Why are they doing this? Why are they singing? Are they singing to me?" I asked.

"This is unbelievable," said the guards. "They are singing to you! They are welcoming you."

"Welcome," they sang lovingly. "You are welcome!"

I absorbed the beauty of this moment and melted in their love for me. I smiled as the crowds joined the caravan. In unison, we continued forward into Baghdad. More than fifty TV cameras from around the world, including China, were waiting and recorded the entry into Baghdad. The sponsors made sure that all vehicles were removed from the main highway so that we were clear to walk. We walked up and over a bridge, the main bridge into the city of Baghdad, and thousands of people were flashing cameras in the daytime.

The city welcomed us. The Iraqi Olympians cried. Never had they been acknowledged with such a welcome.

In front of all the people was a little girl, maybe six years old. She stepped toward me and, looking up, raised a flower to give to me. I bent down to accept her flower. Then I picked her up, turned her around, and set her on my shoulder for the crowds to see this beautiful child. The people went wild and shouted with joy and happiness. My gesture was a message to the world:

"Everyone, see her! This is your child. I love her, you all should love her! She is who I care about. The children, we must protect them."

What a memorable and momentous walk for the children of our world, for the children of Iraq.

Monaco and Prince Albert

After Baghdad, I returned to my command central in Jordan. I was xeroxing some papers in a hotel, and a few ladies who worked there recognized me from the Jordanian media exposure. They were excited and making a little ruckus, in a good way.

"Oh, Mr. Garcia, how can we help you? You don't have to do that. Let us help you. We will make the copies for you." They were so conscientious and went above and beyond to serve me. They treated me with such kindness, like a celebrity.

"Thank you, that is so very kind of you. I will be back for the copies," I said.

A refined gentleman observed all this and was intrigued. He wanted to know who I was.

"He is famous! Don't you know him? He walks around the world for children," the ladies explained.

The gentleman, named Geoffrey, followed me out of the hotel. When he caught up to me, he asked, "Who are you and what do you do?"

Over dinner, I described my walks for children and world peace. After our conversation, Geoffrey invited me to do a walk for the children of France. I said yes, and shortly thereafter I was back in France organizing a walk with Geoffrey, who sponsored the trip and the walk. I remember staying in his home, meeting his lovely and talented wife Martine and their children. Geoffrey volunteered to be my escort driver too.

Geoffrey owned a high-end perfume company, Parfums M. Micallef (named after his wife Martine). They started their perfume house in Grasse at the Côte d'Azur (Cannes) in 1996. Grasse, a town on the French Riviera in the hills north of Cannes, is known for its long-established perfume industry. Geoffrey and Martine have grown their boutique experience of custom perfumes in Europe and the Middle East, and M. Micallef is a signature of high-end luxury. The walk in France involved many people, and it was so successful that Geoffrey talked about doing another walk. They wanted me to walk from Planet Hollywood along the French Riviera and Mediterranean coastline and end at the headquarters of the Red Cross in Monaco.

When I arrived in Monaco, I passed through the prestigious Grand Prix racetrack, through the beautiful villas, and the famous Casino de Monte-Carlo complex and opera house. Monaco is an independent city-state and, although tiny in comparison to its neighbors, is known for elegance and luxury.

After we completed the walk, I was presented a beautiful white book: "Le Livre D'Or De La Croix-Rouge Monegasque" or "The Guest Book of the Monaco Red Cross." It is a privately printed book dedicated by His Serene Highness Prince Albert II, the reigning monarch.

Prince Albert II is also the president of the Monaco Red Cross. He is the son of Prince Rainier III and the American actress Grace Kelly. I found out later that Princess Grace had founded a children's organization called AMADE to promote and protect children morally, physically, and spiritually. Prince Albert wrote me a personal letter thanking me for my love of children.

Along the French Riviera, I connected with a Filipino family who invited me to stay in their home. I accepted their invitation. They were very friendly and worked as caretakers in a French villa just in front of the French Riviera. This family was connected with other Filipinos who also worked in other embassies. They had a good reputation with the dignitaries they worked for. They knew I always loved to pray for people, so they invited me to different places to meet and pray for anyone who needed prayers. It seemed like everyone they knew needed prayers.

LE LIVRE D'OR
DE LA
CROIX-ROUGE
MONÉGASQUE

To Danny Garcia,

Congratulations on your extraordinary accomplishments walking around planet, and doing all this "For the love of Children."

I am so sorry not to meet you personally, but I would like to wish a pleasant stay in Monaco, and on behalf of the Monégasque Red Cross Society and on that of my family; our most sincere and hearty wishes of success! God Bless!

Albert de Monaco

Letter from Prince Albert of Monaco

Crossing the Ponds

I left the French Rivera for the other side of the world, Sydney, Australia, and crossed the oceans several times from one continent to another between 2000–2001. I walked throughout Western Australia and the Philippines.

In Australia, I had native Aborigines as my escorts as I traveled from Perth to Sydney. Also, in Australia, I met Nelson Mandela and presented him a Jubillenium candle in Cambria. Bruce Stephen Foster and I did a concert at Planet Hollywood in Sydney, and an athlete passed by with the Olympic torch during our concert. I also visited the Vatican again during this time. These trips were filled with intrigue and miracles, only mentioned here for brevity. I may expand in another book.

The next story I must tell, though, takes me back to the Middle East for a bold journey in the hot spots of Israel and Gaza.

I feared for my life and called out to God to save me. He covered me with the blood of Jesus.

CHAPTER 13:

Taken Hostage in Gaza

My earlier trips to Israel and Jordan were eye-opening, but not dangerous.

In the Middle East, I experienced people with a strong faith in God. I wanted to do something to bring people together in a peaceful way. That is why I walked. My message to them was "I love you."

God compelled me to go where Jesus walked.

When I loved the people, they responded and opened their countries, their lives, and their hearts. I was accepted as a friend and man of God. I was there to serve them and to pray for my fellow man, walking in unconditional love. I was excited to be with them and to learn everything I could. My excitement was contagious.

This next walk, though, was daring, because the areas I traveled to had ongoing skirmishes, armed conflict, and blockades. I went where others would not go for fear of the dangers lurking. Everyone I told about my walk was concerned for my safety.

"Please reconsider, Danny," they pleaded and cautioned.

"How can I say no to God?" I replied to their objections.

God said, "fear not." I would not allow fear to paralyze me or keep me from my mission.

My quest was to show love to all of them, without choosing a side. I saw the people as precious in the sight of God and treated them with respect.

"Please Save Our Son"

By this time, I was back in Jordan, my command central. The people knew of me through the media. One pastor wanted to introduce me to another Jordanian pastor, so I obliged.

"Danny, we need your help. There is a family, and their young son is very sick. They want to meet you." The pastor described a desperate man who had heard of me and asked for my help.

The man and his wife were Iraqi. Originally, they were trying to reach Jordan's King Abdullah II, and they thought I could connect them to the king for help.

The family of five had moved from Iraq to Libya to work and raise money for a heart operation for their firstborn son. The boy was supposed to have surgery when he was an infant, but they had to postpone the operation until they had enough money. In Libya, their money was stolen. The parents became depressed, so they moved to Jordan in 2000 to find work. Their only concern was the health and survival of their son.

UN representatives told the family they could get free medicine in a clinic located in a church. When the family fled Iraq, they lost their home, their money, and their health. They did not want to lose their son. On Christmas Day of 2000, they decided to go to church. There, they prayed and accepted Jesus. The mother said that their life changed to happiness and peace. They had hope again. The family began to pray in the name of Jesus, asking for help for their son.

"Please, God, send someone to help us," they prayed.

Little did I know that I was the one God would send to be His vehicle of answered prayer. I did not know this Iraqi family, and they did not know me. I met the father in 2001 at the Christian Missionary Church in Amman, and I knew I had to help his son.

When the pastor of the church introduced me to the family, I asked, "How can I help you?"

"When we first came here, we were only concerned about our son's health. We used to sit and pray and call on God to send somebody to help us," said the father. "And, thankfully, God responded."

They explained that their son needed a heart operation and asked for my help. "Please save our son. He is five years old and dying," begged the man.

"I believe God has sent me to help your son. The Lord loves him and wants him to live," I said.

"Are you rich? Do you have the money for our son's operation?" asked the parents.

"No, I am not rich. I walk from country to country for children. God listened to your prayers, and I believe He sent me from America to Jordan to this church. He told me that I have work to do in Jordan."

I then committed (with God's help) to raising money for an operation to correct the tiny malfunctioning valve in the boy's heart. I decided to walk and make known the boy's cause. The route was planned to take me from Jordan through the Gaza Strip.

Why would I, an American, walk for this family? I wanted to show how Christ sacrificed and died that we might live. By example, I continued to plant seeds of God's unconditional love and demonstrated what love is: sacrificial and unselfish. I was prepared for such a time as this, to put my life on the line, and perhaps lose my life, so that a child could live.

In the Middle East, I had to think about the heat and conflict between Israelis and Palestinians. These were constants, and more so in Palestine and the Gaza Strip.

"Danny, please don't go! It is too dangerous," pleaded the father and many others.

We had not raised enough money for the operation, so I went. I had to keep my word. God told me to keep walking because He cares, even if no one else cares or understands. So in June 2001, I set off from Jordan through the Jordan Valley and past the West Bank toward Jerusalem and Gaza.

In the West Bank, a number of Palestinian people met me and brought me to the office of Yasser Arafat in the city of Ramallah. They wanted me to tell their stories of children who had been wounded, maimed, and killed. They told me they would take me to a hotel, arrange for a meeting with leaders in the municipality, and come back for me.

I arrived at the hotel and was given a room on the fourth floor. I began to unpack and get situated.

Suddenly, I heard gunfire coming from the street and firing in the direction of my hotel room. Instinctively, I hit the floor and stayed there in the prone position until the gunfire ceased. It felt like a combat situation, and I had to use my Marine Corps training to survive. It seemed like forever as I waited for the gunfire to stop. When it did, I sat up against the wall and started praying to God. I tried to sleep on the floor but did not get much rest that night thinking about when the next round of gunfire might go off.

The next morning, the Palestinian officials picked me up, gave me food to eat, and took me to a hospital. They showed me some of the kids wounded by guns. The media interviewed me.

I told them, "I walk for these children who are in the crosshairs of conflict."

After the hospital visit, they took me to a building I think was the headquarters of the Palestine Liberation Organization (PLO). Several people welcomed me, and I told them I was walking through Gaza for Palestinian children too. They thanked me, and some of them were weeping as they presented me with a medal on behalf of President Yassar Arafat and the Palestinian children.

I told the representatives where I was going, so the PLO assigned me a security detail of twenty men, ten on each side. The guards walked with me through the Gaza Strip, where I visited several refugee camps. The Palestinians were friendly and grateful that I was walking for their children. At the southern tip of the Gaza Strip, I reached the region of Rafah, which is mostly populated by refugees. Rafah's border crossing, Egyptian-controlled, is the only means of crossing from the Gaza Strip into Egypt. Here, the Palestinian security detail left me. I was alone again.

That afternoon, I arrived in Rafah. As I walked through the streets of Rafah, I felt friction in the air. The tension was thick, hair-raising. I was alone with no escort or entourage. There was no American or UN presence.

The same day, Israeli forces had shot and killed a young Palestinian girl in Rafah. People were in the streets protesting at a heightened pitch. An angry mob of about 2,000 Palestinians saw me walking in the streets. Then three or four of them with rifles grabbed me by my arms. The men pulled me at gunpoint toward a one-story shell of a house.

"Who are you? What are you doing here?" they demanded.

The people in the mob saw everything. They yelled and fired their weapons in the air as if they were cheering my capture. We continued to move toward the building and, once inside, the men shoved me and threw me into a room. I was taken off-guard, dazed.

Then I realized that I was a captive. I had been taken hostage.

Perhaps it was three or four hours? As a hostage, I lost track of time. I relied on my Marine Corps training to survey my surroundings. I was frightened but knew not to show fear or panic. I had to appear calm.

I prayed silently, "Jesus, Jesus, Jesus. You brought me here, you order my every step. I trust you. Keep me calm, give me favor. Save me."

My captors took my backpack and searched through my possessions. They found the silver medal with Arabic writing. They pulled the medal out of my pack like a treasure and held up it.

"What is this?" the captors asked.

Calmly, I said, "I walk for children, and I walk for Palestinian children. That medal was given to me this morning on behalf of Yasser Arafat, expressing his thanks for the walk I am doing for your children."

Yasser Arafat was the Leader of the PLO. Because Mr. Arafat knew of me, the abductors realized they had to protect me, not kill me.

The men quickly repacked and zipped my pack and gave it back to me. They shuffled me from the holding area, took me outside, and threw me into a waiting taxi with my belongings on top of the car.

When the mob saw me being put into a taxi, they turned their attention toward me and ran, charging the taxi. They wanted vengeance to quench their anger at the death of one of their young daughters. They wanted to kill me.

The situation grew more chaotic, and my captors lost control. The bloodthirsty mob swarmed the car, screaming and beating with their fists on all sides. They rocked the taxi side to side, trying to overturn the car to get to me. Would I escape? Would I survive?

I cried out to Jesus, "Help me!"

Covered by the Blood

At that moment, security forces appeared and began to beat the attackers off the taxi to let the car pass. An armed policeman's baton forcefully came down on a man's head. I saw his blood splattered across the windshield, pouring down.

"You are covered by my blood," I heard the Lord say to me.

With white knuckles, we braced ourselves. The taxi jolted forward, and we broke loose from the mob. Down the road, the Palestinians lifted a barricade and we quickly drove what seemed just a few blocks to an Israeli checkpoint. The taxi crossed the checkpoint, and we breathed a sigh of relief. I narrowly escaped my death.

"Danny, this is as far as I can take you. I cannot go further," said the Palestinian taxi driver. I thought it was over with. Then I heard the Israelis.

"Get out of the car," said an Israeli soldier. "Get your gear, throw it to the side, and get up against the wall."

I did exactly what I was told.

This time, it was Israeli soldiers jacking me up. While I was against the wall, with my hands up and pressed flat against the wall, something told me to look backward. I turned my head slowly over my left shoulder. When I turned, I saw a group of six or seven soldiers with automatic weapons, all pointed at me.

"Who are you? Where are you from? Why are you here? Where is your passport?"

"My passport is in my pack," I said calmly.

The soldier looked inside my pack, found my passport, then made some phone calls. After checking me out through Israeli security, he let me go.

"You are OK. Get your gear. It is a brave thing, what you are doing. For you to do this kind of walk in these territories, it is dangerous. I want to thank you, but be careful."

God spared me for yet another day to fulfill His purpose. I crossed into Egypt and continued to Mount Sinai, then to the capital city of Cairo. I kept my Jordanian sponsors aware of my progress. The further I walked and the longer I walked, the more people became aware of the young boy's plight. I walked by the Great Pyramids of Giza and was hosted by a Sheraton hotel for a few days. Then, my sponsors in Jordan arranged a flight for me to return there.

One evening, I went to the church where I met the Iraqi family. The pastor was holding a prayer vigil for the boy who needed the heart operation. After I left the church, I was later told that a stranger had walked to the front and put money into the offering box. The amount put in the box was the exact amount that was needed for the operation. When I heard this, I was so excited! God had answered our prayers; we had the money to do our part for the boy's surgery.

The next morning, I raced to the hospital with great joy to see the boy and share my excitement. When I arrived, the pastor's wife was there. The news she had was upsetting.

"The money that was given from the stranger last night? It was taken and used for another child who needed an operation," she told me.

"How can anybody do that?" I asked. I felt betrayed and thought, "How will the boy survive?"

Dejected, I informed the hospital that I did *not* have the money for the operation. I felt so low, so used. I had to pick myself up. We were short of all the funds required for the doctors' fees.

I knew I had to talk to the director of the hospital and ask for help. So I prayed and asked God for his influence on the hearts of the surgeons.

"Jesus, this is in your hands. You are the great physician. I don't know how, but I believe in faith that you will work another miracle for this Iraqi boy."

And the miracle happened. The Arab hospital had heard about my walk through Jordan, Israel, Gaza, and Egypt. They were moved to give to the cause. In the summer of 2001, the surgeons decided to do the heart surgery for free—no charge! The director of the hospital and all of the surgery team donated their time and services. Wow.

The hospital received great publicity as an in-kind compensation for their generous donation of time and medical services to save the Iraqi boy.

I was there for the surgery. I went to visit the boy, and the staff allowed me inside his room.

"You've got to try to calm him down," the medical team advised me. "The boy is too hysterical. He is fighting us."

I went to the boy's side and encouraged him. "I am going to pray for you. God is helping you, so trust him." The boy calmed down because he trusted me.

"You Need to Get Him More Blood"

The surgery proceeded. During the operation, the head surgeon came out and told me that the boy had used quite a bit of blood.

"Danny, you need to get him more blood," said the surgeon.

"Where? Where do I get blood?" I said to myself, shocked and concerned.

Blood costs money, a lot of money. They told me I could go to the blood bank or the Red Cross. I raced and asked for help, and donations came in. I chose one of the blood providers, and they gave me the cost. I paid for the blood and had it delivered to the hospital.

With the extra blood, the surgeons successfully completed the heart operation. The boy lived. It was a great humanitarian story. The Jordanian newspaper described me as an American veteran, a "globe-trotting philanthropist," an American traveler, and an adventurer who gave an "Iraqi boy a new lease on life."

"My son has been given the gift of life!" exclaimed the father. "It's like waking up from a nightmare that lasted for six whole years. Every night when we went to sleep, we would close our eyes in fear. Thanks be to God. Thank you, Mr. Garcia."

The entire family tangibly experienced the love of Jesus through an American stranger. God worked the miracle, and God saved the boy. The family later journeyed to war-torn Syria, witnessing Christ to Iraqis, Jordanians, and Syrians. Years later, the family found refuge in the United States. What a faithful God.

Jesus helped me to complete my mission. I knew that Jesus saved me to help a young Iraqi boy so that God would be glorified. Those who are willing to lose their life for Christ's sake will indeed find their life, as did I.

I continued promoting peace and looked to God to order my steps. He always gave me signs and direction on where He wanted me to go next. I had grown sensitively aware of how he spoke to me.

I talked to God and said, "I know you want me to walk. I know you want me to pray. Help me to know how to interact with all these people from different countries."

This verse kept me going: "Seek ye first the kingdom of God." Then, God would make the answer known to me.

The answer was love, the consistent love of God. It was love that prompted people to respond.

Being taken hostage was traumatic and had psychological effects on me. I looked back on this event and other close calls in my life. I realized that in every country I visited, my walks were an extension of the challenges and survival that I experienced as a Marine. I remembered other times of troubling ordeals in my life, decades earlier. I remembered what it was like fighting in Spanish Harlem and as a Marine returning from the Vietnam theater to the United States.

Considering these harrowing events, this story now fast-forwards twenty years to when I asked for help to explain my night sweats, flashbacks, and nightmares.

CHAPTER 14:

Transparency and Vulnerability— A Word about PTSD

When I left the Vietnam theater in the 1970s, I returned to the United States broken. I felt rejected and persecuted. I was lost and confused, wanting to be home but scared to be home. How was I supposed to "be?" How was I to be accepted? I never felt truly welcomed, as if I never belonged. No one knew what I had seen, what I did, or knew how I felt inside.

I carried with me the memories of my Marine Corps brothers. I saw the face of Sgt Eaglin, who asked me to be the best man in his wedding. I remembered Sgt Patton, my judo instructor. Both were killed in Vietnam. I knew they were gone but struggled to reconcile the personal loss of my brothers. At home, I wrestled to adapt and to communicate. My family and friends had no understanding of the trauma of war and lost brethren. They were uncomfortable and fumbled with polite questions. There was a distance, a chasm, between us. I felt I was between two completely different worlds.

As a result, I tried to hide. I became quiet. I thought coming home would be safe because I had left a war zone. But I left one war overseas and came back to a nation fighting against each other. Protesters were angry at the US government and saw us as targets for their aggression. We Vietnam veterans were caught in the middle. When I signed up to join the Corps in New York City as a seventeen-year-old kid, I was gung-ho about becoming a Marine and serving my country. I expected the nation to be proud of us, but during the Vietnam War era, they didn't act like they were proud of us. We were ignored. We weren't acknowledged. We were not welcomed home. We were not thanked.

These days, writing in 2020, it is positively different. Whenever I wear my ball cap with the words "Marine Vietnam Veteran," strangers stop me.

They smile and say, "Thank you for your service."

Some say, "Welcome home, Marine." That makes me smile with humility.

They shake my hand with kindness and genuine appreciation. When other Marines see my cap or sweatshirt with the Marine Corps logo, they say, "Semper Fi!" We have immediate camaraderie and can talk so easily to each other. Some call it "old home week" as we swap war stories and tell about where we served and in what units. We relate to each other.

Telling the story of my life and early walks has forced me to recount and relive deep pain. Sometimes, it felt like large scabs were ripped off me, leaving bleeding wounds. I told myself to be transparent, vulnerable, and courageous. In this journey, I have sacrificed myself many times. What drove me to do what I have done? It must have been Jesus telling me, "Go. Don't stop. Don't quit. Follow me." Today, I know who I am and that my existence has mattered. I know who I am in Christ.

Recently, I gained an understanding of *why* I react and respond to crises the way I do. My responses are related to trauma, to conflict such as war.

Many of my fellow veterans have come back from wars and conflicts with afflictions. These afflictions are physical, mental, and spiritual. These days, the term is post-traumatic stress disorder (PTSD). PTSD is not only for those who have been through combat but through any type of trauma (violent crimes or abuse, a devasting natural disaster, terrorist attacks). I've learned that PTSD can result from a consolidation of many separate events. This is called compound PTSD.

Crying on the Inside

Some Marines don't cry on the outside. They really cry on the inside. I have cried many times when I was rejected or betrayed. When I felt alone, hopeless. When I felt overwhelmed, cornered, battered, and used. Being famous is lonely, and I have felt alone many times. Who is your friend? Who can you trust? I only trust my Lord Jesus.

I've seen these afflicted veterans and have even counseled them. I share their pain and have gone through many of their same struggles.

I know because I am one of them.

One day, in 2018, I went to a Veterans Affairs (VA) clinic for a checkup. As standard procedure, the nurses always ask every patient a series of questions. They want to know if we want to hurt ourselves or others, if we have thoughts of suicide, or if we want to talk to a counselor. This day, I thought maybe I should talk to someone.

"Sure, I would like to talk to a counselor," I said.

"OK, if you can wait, we can see you today. Do you want to wait an hour?"

"Yes, I can wait. Thank you."

When I lived in San Diego, I spent many, many years as a drug and rehabilitation counselor. I am a spiritual counselor. I understood the value of counseling. I welcomed it.

"Mr. Garcia?" I heard my name called, then followed the VA psychiatrist into his office. I wanted to know about my night sweats because no other doctor could tell me why I drenched my sheets at night. He asked me a series of questions and I answered him truthfully about how I felt at that moment.

"Do you have flashbacks, vivid memories, or nightmares that make you feel like it is happening all over again?"

"Yes."

"Do you feel constantly on-guard, feel irritated, or have angry outbursts?"

"Yes."

"Are you easily startled?"

"Not particularly."

There were more questions about the use of alcohol and drugs, isolation, and avoidance. He asked about my sleeping habits, my ability to concentrate, and my emotional state. "Mr. Garcia, based on your responses, you have all the signs of PTSD."

Wow. There it was, plain and simple. I paused and thought for a moment to let that statement sink in. I did not know I had it, but it made sense! Finally, I understood why I thought the way I did and acted the way I acted.

Now, in my seventies and as an older man, I asked God, "Lord, what do I do?"

I started to realize that I had certain triggers. Certain people triggered me with their behaviors. Like the way people talk to me, either *at* me or *with* me. If someone is disrespectful or has an attitude and persists in hurting me through words or actions, that's a trigger. I know I must control myself. The street in me comes out. I have had to tame my responses so that someone would not get hurt.

"Don't push me. I'm starting to get pissed off. You don't want me to get angry. Back off."

Sometimes I would just walk away, be silent.

"Leave it all behind. Let it go," I often told myself. "Just walk away."

I did that many times in my life. In fact, I walked around the world and didn't look back.

When I had been walking around the world, I did not have a regular doctor. I was traveling. I was told I had the heart of a twenty-year-old and had walked up to fifty miles a day in my prime.

Because I had not seen a doctor during my years on the road, I really did not know what was going on inside of me. My diet was terrible. I was often thirsty and would drink sodas to quench my thirst. Thinking I should have a general checkup, I made an appointment and had bloodwork done. When I saw the doctor, he was shocked.

"Mr. Garcia, your blood sugar level is severely elevated. Your level is over five hundred. If you had not been walking, you would be dead," explained the doctor.

I was shocked. The doctor told me that my blood was thick like syrup. That is dangerous. I was diagnosed with diabetes and prescribed insulin.

"Will I have this for the rest of my life?"

"Yes," said the doctor. "And you will have to use insulin for the rest of your life too."

I didn't believe it and did not want to accept or claim diabetes. I started the daily regimen of pricking my finger, checking my sugar levels, and shooting insulin into my belly. Then, I began to experience tingling and pain in my feet, especially at night. It felt like someone was sticking needles into my toes and the soles of my feet. Sharp pains would go off like a series of fireworks, attacking the nerves in my feet. This is called peripheral neuropathy, and it is painful.

Sometimes I had episodes of low blood sugar. Breaking into a cold sweat, I would nearly pass out. Most times I caught myself and remained conscious. Diabetes then impacted my eyesight. I had bleeding in my retina and have had many treatments to stop that bleeding to save my eyesight.

Through all of this, nutritionists, doctors, nurses, and pharmacists have advised me. Sometimes they agree. Sometimes they contradict each other. Having to manage diabetes by reducing my blood sugar levels and keeping them consistently stable can be stressful and depressing. Some people just give up. I found a few ways to help.

Exercise and massage keep the blood flowing. I have used essential oils on my feet to ease the pain. For nutrition, I have taken Shaklee vitamins and protein shakes to get the vitamins and minerals I don't get from food. I am learning daily what not to eat or drink. I fight the battle of watching my sugar and intake of carbohydrates. It is exhausting.

I am not perfect. I make mistakes. But I'm trying, and I am not a quitter.

And I will continue to walk until God takes me.

CONCLUSION

The answer to "Have you ever been lost? Really lost?" is a profound reality in this book. We've all been lost and turned to God for hope and redemption.

We owe God everything. God chose an unlikely kid from Spanish Harlem to share spiritual wisdom, inspire, render aid to the needy, and give hope to those in darkness of all kinds.

People on each continent have asked for this book. We are delighted to share the travels, colorful personalities, and extraordinary experiences with the world.

We take no credit. It is all about Jesus.

Young Danny Garcia in New York City (1950)

Danny has prayed and walked more than 52,000,000 steps on six continents.

- Over 26,000 miles, greater than the circumference of the earth

- More than 27 years, beginning on Dec 7, 1996

- Why? For children and world peace

Danny Garcia is the Founder of Global Walk Inc., a Florida Not for Profit Organization. Jacqueline C. Garcia is the CEO and President of Global Walk Inc.

There is a nonprofit organization that embodies Danny's heart and philosophy.

This organization supports Danny and his walks all over the world for charity, children and their families, and world peace.

This organization also honors and thanks God, veterans, first responders, and their families.

The mission of Global Walk Inc. is to
- inspire hope
- share spiritual wisdom, and
- render aid to the needy by walking and praying.

ABOUT THE COAUTHORS

Danny Garcia

Danny Garcia, The Walking Man, was born and raised in New York's Spanish Harlem. He served as a United States Marine, law enforcement officer, and ordained minister. Since 1996, he has prayed and walked over 52,000,000 steps on six continents for children and world peace. During his journeys, Garcia met with dignitaries all over the world, ministering to the  famous and to the poorest of the poor. Danny made presentations to kings/royals, presidents, and other world leaders, including four presidents of the USA, several prime ministers of other countries, the pope, Mother Teresa, ambassadors, and various eminent personalities and multilateral organizations. Garcia began his journey as a personal commitment to peace and children and continued walking and raising funds for multiple charitable organizations.

Danny is married to the former Jacqueline Charsagua of El Paso, Texas, and they work side by side to share the gospel of Jesus Christ. For more information, visit Danny's legacy website, www.globalwalk.cc.

ABOUT THE COAUTHORS

Jackie C. Garcia

Jackie Charsagua Garcia is married to Daniel Garcia. She graduated from the United States Air Force Academy in Colorado Springs, Colorado, in 1985 and was commissioned as a second lieutenant in the United States Air Force. Jackie holds a Bachelor of Science in Management and a Master of Science in Human Resources Management. While in the US Air  Force, Jackie specialized in communications, acquisition, systems engineering, and information technology. After a rewarding and fulfilling Air Force career, she retired as a lieutenant colonel in the summer of 2006, having spent more than twenty-one years on active duty. Since 2006, she has supported and advised on all aspects of her husband's walks and charitable initiatives within the United States and abroad. She joined Danny during his Africa Walk in 2007 and ministered in South Africa, Uganda, Ethiopia, and Southern Sudan. During this time, her faith and reliance on God grew tremendously under the mentorship of Danny Garcia. The Global Walk experience allowed Jackie to serve God abroad, and her vision is to spread the hope, love, and the grace of Jesus Christ through her writing. She is a native of El Paso, Texas, the mother of one amazing daughter, and a breast cancer survivor.

ENDNOTES

Chapter 1

Latin Roots: Afro-Cubans in Spanish Harlem

Greenbaum, Susan D. *More than Black: Afro-Cubans in Tampa.* edited by Kevin A. Yelvington, Gainesville, University Press of Florida, 2002, pp. 144–259.

"Conga." *Wikipedia*, Wikimedia Foundation, 25 Nov. 2019, en.wikipedia.org/wiki/Conga. Accessed 18 Jan. 2020.

Salazar, Max. "Machito, Mario and Graciela: Destined for Greatness." *Latin Beat*, June 1991.

Rosa, Victor Manuel. "Latin Roots Salsa History on Exhibit." Steppin' Out, Aug. 1978.

Austerlitz, Paul. "The Afro-Cuban Impact on Music in the United States: Mario Bauza and Machito." *Music of the United States of America, Volume 26*, edited by Paul Austerlitz and Jere Laukkanen, Middleton, Wisconsin, A-R Editions, Inc., 2016, p. xxv.

Cubob! The Life and Music of Maestro Mario Bauza. edited by Mora J. Byrd, New York, Caribbean Cultural Center, 1993.

Watrous, Peter. "Mario Bauza, Band Leader, Dies; Champion of Latin Music Was 82." The New York Times, 12 July 1993, www.nytimes.com/1993/07/12/obituaries/mario-bauza-band-leader-dies-champion-of-latin-music-was-82.html. Accessed 19 Jan. 2020.

The Copa, Copacabana
"Xavier Cugat." *Wikipedia*, Wikimedia Foundation, 23 Jan. 2020, en.wikipedia.org/wiki/Xavier_Cugat. Accessed 27 Jan. 2020.

Hell's Kitchen
On the Waterfront. Directed by Elia Kazan, Columbia Pictures, 28 July 1954.

Chapter 2
Bridge of Spies. Directed by Steven Spielberg, Touchstone Pictures, 4 Oct. 2015.

Deployed Out to Sea
The Editors of Encyclopedia Britannica. "Cuban Missile Crisis | History, Facts, & Significance." Encyclopedia Britannica, 10 Dec. 2018, www.britannica.com/event/Cuban-missile-crisis.

Thirteen Days. Directed by Roger Donaldson, New Line Cinema, 25 Dec. 2000.

Okinawa, Japan
The D.I. Directed by Jack Webb, Warner Bros., 7 May 1957.

Chapter 3

My Executive Mentor, Bud Roberts
The Secret Life of Walter Mitty. Directed by Ben Stiller, 20th Century Fox, 13 Oct. 2013.

Promoting Woodstock, The Concert

"Woodstock." *HISTORY*, 21 Aug. 2018, www.history.com/topics/1960s/woodstock.

Night Life and Jazz

Theis, David. "Back to the Future." *Downtownhouston.Org*, 2 Sept. 2010, www.downtownhouston.org/news/article/back-future/. Accessed 18 Jan. 2020.

https://forgottenhouston.wordpress.com/2011/07/01/houston-music-scene-the-hippie-years/

"Watermelon Man (Composition)." *Wikipedia*, Wikimedia Foundation, 18 Dec. 2019, en.wikipedia.org/wiki/Watermelon_Man (composition). Accessed 18 Jan. 2020.

Chapter 4

Nam Phong, Thailand

"Royal Thai Air Base Nam Phong." *Wikipedia*, Wikimedia Foundation, 16 Oct. 2019, en.wikipedia.org/wiki/Royal_Thai_Air_Base_Nam_Phong. Accessed 18 Jan. 2020.

"Charles C. Krulak." *Wikipedia*, Wikimedia Foundation, 19 Dec. 2019, en.wikipedia.org/wiki/Charles_C._Krulak. Accessed 27 Jan. 2020.

"Human Relations Makes Garcia's Day"

Humphrey, Robert L. Values for a New Millennium: Activating the Natural Law to Reduce Violence, Revitalize Our Schools, Promote Cross-Cultural Harmony. Maynardville, Tenn., Life Values Press, 2004.

Bohannon, Dennis K. "Human Relations Makes Garcia's Day." *The North Islander*, 25 July 1974, pp. 1, 10.

Leadership Mentor, USMC Major Charles C. Krulak

HQ United States Marine Corps. "ADMINISTRATIVE AND ISSUE PROCEDURES FOR DECORATIONS, MEDALS, AND AWARDS, Marine Corps Order 1650.19J." *Official Website of the United States Marines*, Department of the Navy, 1 Feb. 2001, www.marines.mil/Portals/1/Publications/MCO%20 1650.19J.pdf, Enclosure 2, page 5, Recommendations, Meritorious Mast.

Krulak, CC. "USMC Meritorious Mast." received by Sergeant Daniel Garcia, 12 Mar. 1975. Major Charles C. Krulak, USMC, Commanding Officer, Marine Barracks, Naval Air Station North Island, San Diego, CA.

Chapter 5

Success and Dangerous Indulgences

Row, Abby. "WHO WE ARE - SER National." *Ser-National. Org*, Abby row, 10 Oct. 2016, ser-national.org/who-we-are/. Accessed 23 Jan. 2020.

https://www.drugfreeworld.org/drugfacts/lsd.html

President Carter

Carter, Jimmy. "Thank You, Human Rights Award." received by Daniel Garcia, 12 Oct. 1978. President James E. Carter, Jr., 39th President of the United States.

Diplomatic Mentors, Mr. and Mrs. Alexander

Sparks, Karen. "Sir Eric Matthew Gairy | Prime Minister of Grenada | Britannica." *Encyclopedia Britannica*, 19 Aug. 2019, www.britannica.com/biography/Eric-Matthew-Gairy.

President Carter

History.com Editors. "Carter Signs the Panama Canal Treaty." *HISTORY*, 30 May 2012, www.history.com/topics/us-presidents/carter-signs-the-panama-canal-treaty-video.

"Camp David Accords." *Wikipedia*, Wikimedia Foundation, 19 Nov. 2019, en.wikipedia.org/wiki/Camp_David_Accords.

Little Revelations of God

Strong, Mary. *Letters of the Scattered Brotherhood*. 1948. San Francisco, HarperSanFrancisco, 1991.

Chapter 6

Puebla, Mexico

Warth, Gary. "Dan Garcia's Dream Still May Come True." San Diego Union Tribune, May 1985.

DeYoung, Karen. "1 Million Mexicans and a Mariachi Band Welcome John Paul II." The Washington Post, 27 Jan. 1979.

Strong, Mary. *Letters of the Scattered Brotherhood*, pg. 144

"International Year of the Child." Wikipedia, Wikimedia Foundation, 13 Aug. 2019, en.wikipedia.org/wiki/International_Year_of_the_Child. Accessed 6 Sept. 2019.

Grun, John. "Letter to Certify Presentation and Exhibition of 'The Child' at the UN." received by Agostino Casaroli, 7 Aug. 1980. His Excellency Archbishop Agostino Casaroli, Pro-Secretary of State, Holy See, Vatican City.

Quintana, Pedro Lopez. "Letter of Gratitude, Gifts Presented to Pope John Paul II." received by Daniel Garcia, 26 Jan. 1999. Monsignor Quintana, Assessor, Secretary of State, The Vatican.

Rome, The Vatican

Morrow, Tom. "Noted O'side Businessman, Community Activist Jerry Stapp Dead at 81." San Diego Union-Tribune, San Diego Union-Tribune, 21 Apr. 2006, www.sandiegouniontribune.com/sdut-noted-oside-businessman-community-activist-jerry-2006apr21-story.html. Accessed 20 Jan. 2020.

Chapter 7

The Queen of England

Weber, Dick. "Santee Woman Needs Miracle." The San Diego Union, 21 Jan. 1983, p. B4.

Turegano, Preston. "City Cheers Queen Elizabeth." *The San Diego Union-Tribune*, 26 Feb. 1983, p. 1. Accessed 22 Jan. 2020.

Israel, Prime Minister Shamir and Ancient Masada

Reis, William B. "Concert at Masada Celebrates 40th Israeli Anniversary." UPI, United Press International, 14 Oct. 1988, www.upi.com/Archives/1988/10/14/Concert-at-Masada-celebrates-40th-Israeli-anniversary/9153592804800/. Accessed 18 Jan. 2020.

Rosenberg, Carol. "'Resurrection' to Ring out in Masada." Chicagotribune.Com, 29 Sept. 1988, www.chicagotribune.com/news/ct-xpm-1988-09-29-8802030012-story.html. Accessed 15 Jan. 2020.

President Reagan

US National Archives and Records Administration. "1988 Campaigning for George H.W. Bush | Ronald Reagan Presidential Library - National Archives and Records Administration." Reaganlibrary.Gov, 2019, www.reaganlibrary.gov/photo-galleries/1988-campaigning-for-george-h-w-bush.

Reagan, Ronald. "Thank You Letter, Framed Reproduction of The Child." received by Daniel Garcia, 2 Dec. 1988. President Ronald W. Reagan, 40th President of the United States.

Bosnia

Davis, James. "Task Force Eagle – V Corps Deployment to Bosnia and Logistic Cost." Logistics In War, Logistics In War, 3 Mar. 2017, logisticsinwar.com/2017/03/03/task-force-eagle-v-corps-deployment-to-bosnia-and-logistic-cost/. Accessed 27 Jan. 2020.

"United Nations Mission in Bosnia and Herzegovina." Wikipedia, Wikimedia Foundation, 6 Dec. 2019, en.wikipedia.org/wiki/United_Nations_Mission_in_Bosnia_and_Herzegovina. Accessed 9 Dec. 2019.

Garcia, Daniel. "The Child." KFMB-TV, 8 Jan. 1996. San Diego New Channel 8, Interview by Yvette Dabney.

Nash, William L. "Thank You, Mural Is in Zagreb." received by Daniel Garcia, 16 Jan. 1996. Major General William L. Nash, Commanding General Task Force Eagle.

Chapter 8

"Crucible." Oxford Learner's Dictionaries, Oxford University Press, 2020, www.oxfordlearnersdictionaries.com/us/definition/american_english/crucible. Accessed 18 Jan. 2020.

Half Moon Bay

Trevenon, Stacy. "One Step at a Time for Kids." Half Moon Bay Review, 11 Dec. 1996.

Chapter 9

Domestic Bombings Shake the Nation

"Khobar Towers Bombing in Saudi Arabia Kills 19 U.S. Airmen." *HISTORY*, 12 July 2019, www.history.com/this-day-in-history/saudi-arabia-khobar-towers-bombing-kills-19. Accessed 26 Jan. 2020.

Greenspan, Jesse. "Remembering the 1993 World Trade Center Bombing." *HISTORY*, 26 Feb. 2013, www.history.com/news/remembering-the-1993-world-trade-center-bombing.

"Oklahoma City Bombing." *HISTORY*, 21 Aug. 2018, www.history.com/topics/1990s/oklahoma-city-bombing. Accessed 20 Jan. 2020.

Warren, Carl. "Putting His Feet ... Where His Mouth Is." Marshall News Messenger, 24 Mar. 1997, p. 1B.

Hammer, Jo Lee. "Walk Memorializes Bombing Victims." Longview News-Journal, 23 Mar. 1997, p. 2A.

The Unexpected, A Day in the Life

Hazel, Diane. "Former Marine Walks in Memory of Children." *Denton Record-Chronicle*, 28 Mar. 1997, pp. 11A, 12A.

President Clinton

Fournier, Ron. "Clinton Hurts Right Knee in Fall at Golfer Greg Norman's Home." AP NEWS, Associated Press, 14 Mar. 1997, apnews.com/89bf9c838e95af4ec5384d33eae8f3ce. Accessed 27 Jan. 2020.

Thompson, Mary Jane. "Yes Indeed, He's Walking." Times Newspapers, 25 June 1997, pp. 72–73.

Clinton, Bill. "Thank You, Walking Stick and Video." received by Daniel Garcia, 2 July 1997. President William J. Clinton, 42nd President of the United States.

USMC Tank Escort on Atlantic City Boardwalk

Public Affairs Office, Recruiting Station New Jersey. "George Washington Bridge Crossing Represents Final Footsteps of San Francisco to New York Walk for Children but Just Begins Global Walk." USMC Recruiting Command, Recruiting Station New Jersey, Public Affairs Office, 30 June 1997. Press Release 97–05.

Gomez, Javier. "Por Amor a Los Ninos." *El Diario La Prenza*, 10 July 1997, p. 6.

"Princess Diana Dies in a Car Crash." *HISTORY*, 29 Aug. 2019, www.history.com/this-day-in-history/princess-diana-dies-in-car-crash-paris. Accessed 27 Jan. 2020.

Super Bowl XXXII, Danny Garcia Day

Oravetz, Janet. "9 Facts about the 1998 Super Bowl." *USA TODAY*, 30 Jan. 2016, www.usatoday.com/story/sports/nfl/denver-broncos/2016/01/29/9-facts-about-the-1998-super-bowl/79545578/.

tenBerg, Yvette. "One Step at a Time: San Diegan Walks World for Children." *La Prensa San Diego*, 22 Feb. 2002.

Krulak, C.C. "Letter of Congratulations, Walk Across America." received by Daniel Garcia, 26 June 1997. General CC Krulak, USMC, 31st Commandant of the Marine Corps.

Hoboken, Walk for "Blue Eyes"

DeAngelis, Martin. "He Does It His Way -- by Walking." The Press of Atlantic City, 31 July 1998.

King Hussein I of Jordan

Hussein I. "Thank You, Get Well Wishes and Gifts." received by Daniel Garcia, 30 Aug. 1998. His Majesty King Hussein bin Talal, King of Jordan.

Chapter 10

United States Marine Band. "SOUSA Hands Across the Sea (1899) - 'The President's Own' United States Marine Band." YouTube, 9 Apr. 2018, www.youtube.com/watch?v=W4x3LFlnfcg. Accessed 28 Jan. 2020.

Masko, David. "Marine's Journey Takes Him Far: Vietnam Veteran Walks to Heal." The Stars and Stripes, 13 Sept. 1998, p. 3.

Scotland Yard on Duty

"Omagh Bombing." *Wikipedia*, Wikimedia Foundation, 24 Nov. 2019, en.wikipedia.org/wiki/Omagh_bombing.

Scotland, The Royal Marines

Dalton, KD. "Once a Marine Always a Marine, Hands Across the Sea." received by Daniel Garcia, 1 Oct. 1998. Warrant Officer 2 KD Dalton, Royal Marines.

Forrest Gump. Directed by Robert Zemeckis, Paramount Pictures, 24 June 1994.

Cowan, Mark. "'Real Grump' Walks into Brum." *Birmingham Evening Mail*, 12 Oct. 1998.

Rolston, Henrietta. "Thank You, Walking Stick Gift for Prince of Wales." received by Daniel Garcia, 5 Nov. 1998. Office of HRH The Prince of Wales.

Netherlands, The Dutch Marines

Ray, Michael. "The Hague | History, Geography, Court, & Points of Interest." *Encyclopedia Britannica*, 28 Sept. 2017, www.britannica.com/place/The-Hague. Accessed 14 Aug. 2019.

International School of Geneva

Samuel, Luanne. "Visit of Danny Garcia to the International School of Geneva." received by Maria Stoy, 10 Dec. 1998. L. Samuel, Coordinatrice des Relations Extérieures, École Internationale de Genève.

Hungary and Italy

"Frei Tamas." *Wikipedia*, 13 May 2019, hu.wikipedia.org/wiki/Frei_Tamás. Accessed 21 Jan. 2020. Translated from Hungarian version of Wikipedia.

Frei, Tamas. "Letter of Request to Film Danny Garcia's Presentation to Pope John Paul II." received by James Harvey, 7 Dec. 1998. Bishop James Harvey, the Vatican.

Chapter 12

Olmert, Ehud. "Letter of Congratulations, Unique Message of Peace and Children's Rights." received by Daniel Garcia, 11 Jan. 1999. Ehud Olmert, Mayor, Municipality of Jerusalem.

The Hashemite Kingdom of Jordan

"Aqaba Special Economic Zone Authority." *Wikipedia*, Wikimedia Foundation, 3 Feb. 2019, en.wikipedia.org/wiki/Aqaba_Special_Economic_Zone_Authority. Accessed 29 Jan. 2020.

Hashemite Kingdom of Joran, Ministry of Youth. "Cooperation in the Field of Youth Programs in Jordan." received by Daniel Garcia, 29 Jan. 1999. Amman, Jordan.

Who Is My Neighbor?

Qummi, Shaikh Abbas. "Hospitality Toward Guests." Al-Islam.Org, Ahlul Bayt Digital Islamic Library Project, 1995, www.al-islam.org/characteristics-muslim/hospitality-toward-guests. Accessed 17 Sept. 2019. Shaikh Abbas Qummi.

Chapter 13

"Please Save Our Son"

"Rafah." *Wikipedia*, Wikimedia Foundation, 15 Jan. 2020, en.wikipedia.org/wiki/Rafah. Accessed 22 Jan. 2020.

"You Need to Get Him More Blood"

Al Wakeel, Dina. "Globe-Trotting Philanthropist Give Iraqi Boy New Lease on Life." Jordan Times, 22 July 2001.

Chapter 14

Leonard, Jayne. "What to Know about Complex PTSD." *Medical News Today*, Medical News Today, 28 Aug. 2018, www.medicalnewstoday.com/articles/322886.php.

Danny returns to Half Moon Bay

Contact the Coauthors
Danny Garcia and Jackie C. Garcia
Email: globalwalk7@gmail.com

We Salute You
Sgt Danny Garcia, USMC
Lt Col Jackie C. Garica, USAF (Ret.)